*At the Pines*

*At The Pines*, by Max Beerbohm

# MOLLIE
# PANTER-DOWNES

# AT THE
# PINES

*SWINBURNE AND WATTS-DUNTON*
*IN PUTNEY*

**HAMISH HAMILTON**
**LONDON**

*First Published in Great Britain 1971*
*by Hamish Hamilton Ltd*
*90 Great Russell Street London W.C.1*

SBN 241 01943 5

© *by Mollie Panter-Downes 1971*


*Most of this book was first published*
*in 1971 in* The New Yorker

*Printed in Great Britain by*
*Western Printing Services Ltd Bristol*

To Clare

# Acknowledgments

I must express my deep gratitude to Mrs. Edith Saunders, the owner of The Pines, who (with her late husband) gave me every help and showed so much kindness to me and interest in this book.

I would also like to thank the following for helpful conversations or suggestions: the late Mrs. Helen Angeli Rossetti and her daughter, Mrs. Geoffrey Dennis; Mr. R. Dixon of the Brixton School of Building; Mr. William Gaunt; Mrs. Virginia Surtees; Mr. Oliver Warner; Dr. Michael Wolff, editor of 'Victorian Studies', Indiana University, and Mr. Charles Williams.

# List of Illustrations

# I

ONE SPRING day in 1899 a slight and, one may be
sure, elegantly dressed young man emerged, an
unlikely butterfly, from the drab brick edifice of the
South Western Railway Station at Putney, which normally
traffics in more grub-like characters, and drifted slowly
across the Upper Richmond Road to where the slope of
Putney Hill begins to climb towards the Heath. He was in
no hurry. The house towards which his lingering footsteps
were taking him was only a moderately vigorous stone's
throw away; he has left it on record that he could have
wished it further. Max Beerbohm was on his way to lunch
with Theodore Watts-Dunton, an acquaintance he encountered from time to time in London literary drawing-
rooms, and he would have welcomed a little calming exercise to help him prepare his thoughts for the great occasion.
It was not the prospect of conversing with Watts-Dunton in
his own instead of somebody else's drawing-room that was
agitating Beerbohm, but he had been expressly invited to
'come down to Putney' and meet his host's house-mate for
the last twenty years, Algernon Charles Swinburne. In
prose as carefully chosen, as delicately blended as his attire
undoubtedly was that day, he has since described for us how
haltingly, even reluctantly, he approached the house where
he was to partake of luncheon with a legend.

Come down to Putney! The phrase suggests something of
an expedition, a trek into the backwoods where the natives

might or might not be friendly. It was so, Beerbohm has told us, that, when he was young, many people regarded those outlandish places to which one journeyed on the suburban line of the South Western Railway. Fifteen years later, in 1914, when Swinburne had been dead five years and Watts-Dunton was to follow him that June when all their world and much of Beerbohm's was about to be swept away in the first slide of the avalanche, he published his account of the luncheon party in an essay 'Number 2, The Pines'. He tells us that it was held at the time to be highly humorous that Swinburne, the dazzling boy whose wondrous singing had electrified his generation, lived in one of the then despised, over so slightly common suburbs. Born into the landed aristocracy, staunchly pagan in his beliefs, he had disappeared into Pooter Land, where the wine is apt to be Jackson *Frères* and the conversational air is stuffy. Muffled by plush, his voice had changed its note. To Beerbohm, now with his hand on the garden gate, this geographical placing of the poet presented no difficulty. What caused him to toy for one fearful moment, he says, with the thought of flying even now from the meeting, was the marvellous but disturbing notion that Swinburne should exist anywhere, in however altered or muted a form. The extraordinary being who had flashed across the astonished vision of Henry Adams in 1863 at a week-end houseparty at Monckton Milnes' house, Fryston Hall, in Yorkshire—the 'tropical bird', Adams described the apparition, 'high crested, long beaked, quick moving, with rapid utterance and screams of humour, quite unlike any English lark or nightingale', shrilling a torrent of Shakespeare, Dante, Sophocles, Villon, and his own lyrics—had become a fabled phoenix more durable and easier to believe in, on the whole, than the still living, deaf old man who for so long had found a nest in the eaves of The Pines.

As it turned out, there appeared to be no drawing-room in the frowsty but cosy establishment of the two friends in the semi-detached villa on Putney Hill. All but one of Beerbohm's visits, he tells us in the famous essay (for the invitation is repeated), are confined to the dining-room. Once he is taken upstairs after lunch to Swinburne's library to be shown his books. At the dining-room table, Watts-Dunton carves a huge joint of mutton, and Swinburne sits silently (to the guest's disappointment) smiling at his plate and at his precious allowance of one small bottle of Bass's pale ale that stands before him. Even Jackson *Frères* does not flow here, in case it should tempt him to upset the healthful curriculum imposed by Watts-Dunton all those years ago, when the poet was rescued by his friend, like the hero of a Victorian street ballad, from a drunkard's death. 'Please sell no more drink to my father / It mikes 'im so queer and so wi-hild'. Swinburne, eking out his little bottle, is wild no longer, but queer in an elfin way—yes. Beerbohm takes in with the mutton every detail of the 'strange small figure in grey, having an air at once noble and rogueish, proud and skittish', who looks fatter than he is because he carries himself 'with his long neck strained so tightly backwards that he all receded from the waist upwards'. He sits exiled behind the plate-glass partition of his deafness. Up to a point, that is. The luncheon formula on every occasion proves to be the same. After the joint has gone out, assisted by an anonymous cap and apron who is present, the apple pie enters. The whole room must have been impregnated richly with those two excellent English smells. At this stage, and no other, Swinburne is given his cue into the conversation by Watts-Dunton, who bellows, 'Well, Algernon, how was it on the Heath to-day?' And cooingly, Beerbohm recalls, in 'a frail sweet voice' and 'a flow of words so right and sentences so perfectly balanced that they would have seemed

3

pedantic had they not been clearly as spontaneous as the wordless notes of a bird in song', Swinburne tells them of the wonders he has encountered that morning in his habitual healthful walk on Putney Heath.

Max Beerbohm drew Swinburne later on several times as his younger self—the tiny red haired Algernon, no higher than a pepper-pot and as fiery, perched arrogantly among the lumbering fleshy shapes of Dante Gabriel Rossetti and his friends, who sprawl around on the furniture like beached seals. They listen gloomily while Algernon declaims his poetry, one little hand sawing the air, doll boots dangling. Sometimes he wears a funny conical top hat, with a brim so invisible that it looks like a fez, perched in his great fuzz of curls. The voice one fancies one hears from these drawings is no coo. It is the screech of that exotic fowl Henry Adams noted long ago startling the clear air of Yorkshire. Then, finally, there is the touching drawing at the Ashmolean of Swinburne and Watts-Dunton in old age at The Pines. The burning bush of locks, which some contemporaries saw as gleaming gold but a cousin unromantically remembered as plain 'red, violent, aggressive red', has burnt itself out and left bare the huge domed mount of the poet's head. Still leaning backwards, his little feet in carpet slippers pointing neatly outwards like those of a child in dancing class holding the 'first position', he is emphasizing some remark with a finger poked into Watts-Dunton's crumpled frock-coat. Watts-Dunton, also slippered, seems to have lost little of his foliage. The shaggy moustache cascades from his upper lip as though from a balcony window-box, but the under-pinnings of the building—his baggy trouser knees—are sagging. The two friends, inclining vaguely together as if grown into each other out of long habit in an alliance more vegetable than human, are being studied from the wall of The Pines by a vast Rossetti woman—it is surely Jane

4

Morris, the beautiful wife of William Morris—with a neck as long and columnar as Algernon's own. She is gazing down from her frame at the old men with an inscrutable expression, one of her heavy lidded eyes showing ever such a slight disposition to wander off to the left-hand corner as though expectant of seeing Dante Gabriel enter. But he had never made the expedition to Putney. For some rather mysterious reason he had quarrelled with Swinburne seven years before the move to The Pines, and three years later, still with the estrangement left miserably unsettled, he was dead.

I have often read and thought about Max Beerbohm's account of the household of the two friends at The Pines. It is so delightful, so good-humoured and affectionate, that now and then I asked myself whether the picture is not, perhaps, slightly tinted, as delicately as the wash of wild-flower water-colours tints the marvellous drawings, by the good-humour and warmth of Sir Max's own heart. For various friends of Swinburne, I knew, had viewed it through distinctly less flattering glasses. Sir Edmund Gosse's 'Life' of the poet mentions Watts-Dunton, when it is unavoidable, with icy decorum. A critic called Clement Shorter caused much umbrage among Watts-Dunton's friends after his death by referring nastily, in an article in *The Sphere*, to 'Swinburne's premature senility in that terrible *ménage* at The Pines [which] led to a literary as well as a moral deterioration'. There were other uncharitable hints dropped by contemporaries that differed a good deal, I seemed to recall, from Sir Max's recollections of the Victorian villa and 'the two dear old men that lived there'.

*Where* was suddenly revealed to me one day, a year or so ago, when, happening to be in Putney, I read on the stone pillars of an iron front gate, somewhat obscured and overpowered in the general confusion of buildings surrounding

5

the cross-roads where the residential Hill meets with the shopping baskets and perambulators of the High Street, in letters as clearly incised as though they were chipped yesterday: 'THE PINES'. I had somehow remained ignorant of the fact that it might have survived the onslaughts of the armies of well-to-do, impersonal modern blocks of flats that march up Putney Hill, supplanting the big old houses in their pleasant gardens that in not so hoary living memory stood there, the stampede of the super-markets, the various widening and flattening plastic operations performed upon the face of the neighbourhood so that the stertorous breathing of the traffic may be briefly easier. I found myself looking over the gate at the house, standing in such Victorian rectitude beside its semi-detached neighbour, and in stupefaction addressing it, as though startled into the naïve by a celebrated personage unexpectedly encountered in strange surroundings: 'Not *The* Pines?'

To which the house seemed to point mutely and a shade reproachfully to the customary pious decoration bestowed on the homes of distinguished Londoners, the round Wedgewood-blue plaque, awarded here by the old London County Council in (I learnt later) 1926. 'Algernon Charles Swinburne, poet (1837–1909) and his friend Theodore Watts-Dunton, poet, novelist and critic (1832–1914) lived and died here', the medallion proclaimed to any of us who might care to pause and tread water in the strong mid-morning current of Putney comings and goings, to gaze into the little backwater where the remarkably well-preserved relict sat quietly above the noise of the present rushing by in a myriad flooding channels of life. A widow who had outlived two husbands, she seemed to contemplate me back with the withdrawn expression of one whose memories are now inhabited by ghosts, while primly ignoring the anomalies of her new position—the dentist's

6

brass plate on the gate-post of her neighbour, otherwise almost a twin to herself; beyond that, a launderette promising a miraculously speedy return of clean shirts; and looming above her on the other side, the crowding blocks of flats set round with their bright parterres of parked cars, appearing to crane rather hungrily over the wall into the garden space I could not see but imagined at the back.

It was impossible, of course, that I should fail to see ghosts here too, in a sort of double vision, a haunting within a haunting, like a series of small, enthralling carved boxes that fit one inside the other. First, I must picture the slender young man, Max, standing diffidently with his hand on the heavy black iron gate, while past him went the carelessly whistling, enviable butcher boy, happily unencumbered by anything more alarming than the task of delivering yet another leg of mutton of Victorian amplitude to some less eminent household further up the Hill, who was not about to have lunch with Swinburne. Then the sight of the massive mahogany front door with its dignified bronze knob, knocker, and aperture for letters—all announcing 'I am hand wrought, I know not the machine'—made me think of the thousands of times it must have opened to eject a small red-haired figure who proceeded, then and there, to march out briskly through the observant form of Max and disappeared at a fine rate among the oblivious passers-by in the direction of the Heath. Finally I seemed to make out, lurking behind the white net curtains that screened the ground-floor bow-window, ornamented by a classic mask of a horned and bearded satyr which was complemented by the head of some benevolent marine deity above the matching window of the sister house, the frock-coated shape of the second inmate of The Pines. That walrus-moustached face, peering out from the aquarium depths, was certainly

7

watching for Algernon, who had been walking in the rain and was already two minutes beyond his normal clockwork return for luncheon.

The discreet white curtains signalled reassuringly to me that the house had managed to avoid any truck with commerce, a new fate often befalling London houses in which by day dwell filing-cabinets, typewriters, and girls brewing pots of office tea, and which by night are given up to ghosts, too, and moonlight spilling in through uncurtained windows onto the floors. It was neither offices, nor, thank goodness, a 'shrine', religiously preserved as a period place, where I could pay to enter and spend half an hour or so mooning round its literary past. Perhaps protected by its blue plaque, like a virtuous character presented with a magic cloak in a fairy-tale, it had remained itself among all the changes and the predatory excavators—at this moment, I had noticed, biting and grabbing away on the other side of Putney Hill, where a technical college was due to arise. The Pines was still, it seemed, a house where people lived. I craned my neck upwards to look at the odd little tower that sat on top of the building, a widow's toque trimmed with curlicues of jetty-black iron railings, from the crown of which, stiff as aigrettes, stuck up some T.V. aerials. But where, I asked myself, were the trees that had given the twin houses their name? There are pines up on Putney Heath, but the largest tree in Swinburne's 'bleak, trim front garden', as Beerbohm recalled it—still bleak and trim today—was a miniature weeping ash, of tortuous, urban, and faintly Oriental appearance. Unless they were in the invisible back garden, they must have perished in some municipal bout of widening and flattening, I was thinking, when it dawned on me, very belatedly, that the name referred to the ornaments crowning the gate pillars—a pair of handsome stylized pineapples, stone portraits of the exotic which would be

8

brought home from Covent Garden by a City gentleman, swaddled tenderly from the foggy air in blue tissue-paper, to make the centre-piece of the silver or rosy glass *épergne* at his dinner-party. The gate of the neighbouring house where the dentist lived had lost its pines and appeared diminished. Though the old name had been left on the pillars of Swinburne's house, both it and its twin, I noted, had also been obliged to part with their old rural double identity which Beerbohm has preserved forever in his title. The Pines, the famous second one, added the information that it was now Number 11, Putney Hill, to the postman, though not to me.

I wondered who lived in this house that in my imagination was so full to overflowing of Swinburne and Watts-Dunton that the notion could only be of a stranger perched rather uneasily on top of the rich accumulation of associations and evocative loose ends, like a cuckoo sitting in the nest of two small and indignant birds. It became such an imperative demand that, quite soon after the first encounter, I had enquired here and there, and was, as a consequence, calling one late afternoon on the owner of The Pines—a lady who did not live there at all, but in a far prettier Victorian house not far distant. She was charmingly sympathetic. The custody of a house awarded one of the magical blue medallions imparts a large sense of hospitality, it seems; Swinburnian pilgrims arrived on its doorstep from time to time, she said, usually armed with cameras. She and her husband (he had died only recently) had both loved antique furniture and houses, she told me; the evidence was gracefully all round us in the room. They had loved The Pines, the long leasehold of which they had bought in 1960, sufficiently to contemplate at one time moving with their precious pieces (but it turned out that there would not be enough space) into its principal flat. For its serene, white-veiled assurance to me of being still marvellously all of a piece among the surrounding stress and strains, still the unravished bride of quietness undisturbed since first Swinburne and then Watts-Dunton regrettably disappeared, turned out to be not altogether true. Its owner explained that the house had been cut up into three flats, which she let furnished, by her predecessors, a doctor and his wife. The tenants of the ground and first floors, a South African broadcasting man and his family, had just moved out, she said, and it happened that she was on her way there now to take notes of any needed re-decorating and to look through the linen-cupboard. I was invited to accompany her and made free of The Pines, to wander at will while she was thus engaged.

When that solid front door had opened to the owner's key and shut behind us with a weighty deliberation, a thoughtful thump which seemed to stretch much distance between us in the little entrance lobby and the first rush of the usual evening chariot-race of commuters' cars belting noisily up Putney Hill, the silence of the place said instantly 'Not at home'. The Pines was alone, from tower to cellar; the tenants of the top and basement flats, my companion remarked as she unlocked the inner front door of the ground floor, would not yet have returned from business. And it is difficult for us to feel at home either, the plaintive resident ghosts occasionally confided in my ear as I wandered through the good, high ceilinged rooms that instantly challenged a fond pilgrim to try, like an interior decorator reproducing the period his client's belongings require, to slap thick brown layers of atmosphere, incrustations of fustiness and mustiness as deep as a costly flock-patterned paper, over the shocking lightness and levity of their walls. Modern cheerfulness had, of course, long since broken in here, banishing the elaborate old tiled fireplaces, the patterned dadoes, and the gas brackets, and substituting, for the draped and cluttered objects that my mind's eye had gone on obstinately providing, the comfortable but anonymous furnishing of a domestic scene staged for a series of flitting strangers. Her tenants, the owner mentioned before departing to count sheets, had included a well known group of young pop musicians, whose practice sessions must have dislodged those uneasy household spirits some more, and a visiting professor from, more suitably, the department of Victorian studies at Indiana University, who had settled happily here for a sabbatical year.

Yet, I felt, the absence now of all personal possessions in the swept and garnished rooms, their air of submissively waiting for something or somebody to tell them who they were, as a patient suffering from loss of memory might glance up hopefully at a newcomer approaching his bed, was a help in the task of filling the blankness with what one liked. Little clues to the lost past shyly jogged one's elbow here and there. One failed rather badly, it was true, in Swinburne's library on the first floor back, the room where the recall ought to have been strongest, to do away with the anachronistic wash-basin and dressing-table and capacious wardrobe of its present incarnation as a place for sleeping in, not reading or writing. The clean, cheery wallpaper resolutely refused to be covered with shelves of dim bindings and untidy stacks of manuscripts written on Swinburne's special blue paper. But the door, like every door in the house, repeated on its brass handles and plates the careful craftsmanship of the fittings of the front door; the mahogany balustrade, even on a staircase sadly reduced in width by the necessity of fitting in behind a new partition wall the flight of separate stairs to the topmost flat, called modest attention to the fact that it was good, honest mid-Victorian stuff, not to be found in any of the upstart blocks of flats

11

about the place. Only in the tiny tower-room, where a water-tank gurgled, to which I climbed by a narrow ladder-like flight, did the true smell of The Pines appear to be concentrated—a dry, ancient whiff of an age which seemed to have risen to the top of the house and stayed there, as the aroma of roasting mutton and of apples stewing gently with their attendant cloves must have floated up so often from the dark domain of the whisking caps and aprons.

Most of all, perhaps, in the long pleasant strip of garden, led down to by the verandah steps on which Swinburne stood to pose in his braided frock-coat and Bohemian wide felt hat for a photograph in 1889, the site came to life and admitted knowledge of him and Watts-Dunton. 'A good garden', Beerbohm had called it. It was still good, in its countryfied old way, with its fruit trees and shabby potting-shed, its patch of vegetable garden beyond the flower-beds where grew (it was early winter) only a blackened summer refugee from some runner bean vines and a few crowns of purgative rhubarb. In the failing blue light I trod, and nearly lost my footing, on hundreds of small yellow-brown pears that lay, thick as hailstones after a storm, and still hardily un-rotten, under the big central tree before which, in its sapling days, used to stand the plaster statue of the Vatican Venus brought from Rossetti's garden at 16, Cheyne Walk. The Venus had departed, but a nostalgic iron garden seat remained. The huge ferns I remembered seeing in photographs, which had come, I had read, from Watts-Dunton's old home at St. Ives in Huntingdonshire, had gone, and so had the border of iris, the common purple 'flags' that will flourish sturdily in the thin London soil and lift up their splendid heads faithfully like Persian princes defying the skirmishing tribes of London cats. Roses were planted here, but what had happened, I wondered, to the

12

old-fashioned bush which had the charming name of Hebe's Lip and used, I had read, to garland the little Venus? *Rosa damascena rubrotincta*, I later discovered Hebe's less romantic name to be in a modern rose catalogue, which promised that she would be creamy-white and gloriously full, stained deep pink at the base of the petals and redolent of the faint, delicious perfume of her ancestress, the wild dog-rose of the English hedgerows. This true poet's rose had absconded too, it seemed. Yet, with tenacious herbaceous loyalty, the garden was the same, even if the house was not.

Before I went back to the house, where lights now showed, I recalled another of those splendid Victorian photographs that so often, in the unadorned integrity of their rich, matt black and white, surprise us by seeming to tell us more about the originals than their grand portraits do when we seek them out in museums or college halls and stand questioning before them, trying to separate the faces from the fine painting of academic hood and gown, or a gold-braided jacket, or the judicial scarlet. The photographer from Putney had taken Swinburne and Watts-Dunton in the garden of The Pines, sitting facing each other on ordinary wooden house chairs, the legs of which are planted in quite long grass powdered with daisies. They have bowler hats set firmly on their heads, and they do not look comfortable. Swinburne loved nature in the wild, and so did Watts-Dunton, but neither of them was a garden man. They preferred indoors, good book-cases, and not too much air to blow papers about. Their sober dark figures, communing so closely that their knees almost touch, look like passengers helping each other to while away the tedium of a trying railway journey, with the windows tight shut against the passing summer day, which they are ignoring. And it pleased me to leave them there in fancy, forever projected

13

as though from an old magic lantern against the screen of a tall hedge which also seemed to have perished with the iris, the ferns, and Hebe's Lip in some unrecorded, distant floral massacre, joined in their long domestic union, so oddly connubial, at The Pines.

## II

T HE PINES was built on land that was part of the
Lime Grove property of Sir Francis Rose, baronet,
of Penn, Buckinghamshire. The estate took its name
from the large mansion, long vanished, where Edward
Gibbon was born in 1737. About 1870, Sir Francis sold the
Putney Hill site to a builder, John James Spink, of Upper
Richmond Road. The railway had arrived twenty odd years
before. Putney had razed most of its aristocratic past and
was shrewdly building comfortable middle-sized villas to
attract City men who liked to go home in the evenings to
clean air and rural peace. Mr. Spink was busy elsewhere in
the neighbourhood, judging by houses very like The Pines,
sometimes adorned with similar large, cool classical faces,
which can still be encountered in a walk round the side
streets. It was the period of Victorian romanticism which
enjoyed gods and goddesses and their entourage. The residential streets manage to keep something of their old character to-day. In spring, lilacs and laburnums hang over the
walls of occasionally doggedly eccentric houses that feature
windows with stained glass lozenges set in tortured panes,
and built-out landing nooks destined, one thinks, for difficult bits of furniture or grandfather clocks, and perhaps a
romantic turret of doubtful utility. Carriage mews preserve
a rumour of the horse among their rows of garages. Black-
birds sing lustily in well established trees, and now and then
a dog in a parked car stiffens and looks apoplectic as a

15

squirrel, in no great hurry, bounds across the road. The country atmosphere is faint but pursuing.

Swinburne was forty-two when he moved to Putney in 1879. Walter Theodore Watts, as he then was (for it was not until 1896 that he tacked on his mother's maiden name of Dunton by deed poll and hyphen, apparently to meet the terms of some family legacy), was five years older. To Swinburne's eye, which had the cheerfulness of returning good health after a trip to the very doors of the tomb, Putney Hill had the air of 'the outlying (and prettiest) parts of Oxford'. It was the note he wished to sound for himself. None of those ill-natured sneers about banishment to the suburbs, but the charming thought of an academic retreat, not more than a comfortable distance from good friends such as Ned Burne-Jones, Edmund Gosse, or William Rossetti, from the museums and the booksellers. To drive to Hyde Park Corner took an hour. In October, all his possessions— one vanload, including the furniture that had been in his rooms at Balliol and had followed him round, like faithful hounds, to his various London lodgings, one or two family portraits, and his precious books—had made the reverse journey and trundled across the river to The Pines from his last London address at 25, Guildford Street, Russell Square. The decorations at Number 2 were not yet finished, so for a few weeks he and Watts-Dunton camped out with a few belongings next door in Number 1, which was also empty. Swinburne ran up and down the stairs of their new home and swarmed, as nonchalantly as any squirrel, along a ladder from the tower room on to the leads of the roof, where he pronounced the view of the surrounding houses and leafy gardens, the haze of city smoke hanging low in the sky beyond the Thames, the Heath rising towards open country to the south, 'really very nice'. He had always had an excellent strong head for heights, but this would be the domestic

16

scale of his climbing feats from now on. It was his pride to remember that in his youth at Bonchurch, in the Isle of Wight, where he used to ride and swim and visit happily back and forth with a nearby houseful of lively young cousins, he had perilously climbed a hitherto impregnable cliff, just to see if it could be done. He was always testing his physical courage, to prove something or other to himself. Five feet four and a half inches high, afflicted with a nervous system so highly strung that his short arms and legs jerked as though manipulated by strings, he had wanted as a boy to be a soldier, to enter the Dragoons. Or was that another self-fantasy, like his assertion in middle age to a friend that 'of all things' he would have liked to be the keeper of an isolated light-house? The sea, true enough, was his native element. He threw himself into it in all weathers, as naturally as the sea-gulls with whom it pleased him to claim co-sanguinity. Eleven years before he emerges on the Putney leads, he had swum so far out while on holiday at Étretat that he was swept off by the current and only providentially hooked out, a half-drowned morsel, by the crew of a French fishing smack, who became, to a man, his admiring friends and the following year took him out fishing for octopus. He might have died like Shelley, but instead, here he was about to settle down at The Pines. Really very nice. A note of determination sounds here, as though the mild suburban scene can be made to suffice agreeably for a larger lost canvas.

And soon, when he and Watts have moved into their own house and books are lying everywhere in hopeless confusion on the floor of his new library, we find him writing to his old friend and worldly mentor, Richard Monckton Milnes (now Lord Houghton, still the cynically amused and amusing correspondent for whose benefit Swinburne's letter-writing style unbuttons itself, puts its feet on the table, and becomes thankfully bawdy from time to time):

17

'Here I am, like Mr. Tennyson at Farringford, "Close to the edge of a noble down".' This is going it somewhat, but no matter. It is yet another of those consoling manoeuvres of the fancy, like the thought of his small, frail person winning glory in the Dragoons; like the wistful ambition to be a lighthouse keeper, all alone, surrounded by the marvellous green and blue meadows of the sea, master of the light and his own soul. So Mr. Tennyson could stalk, twitching his cloak, over his noble down on the Isle of Wight, and Mr. Swinburne would have Putney Heath and the neighbouring Wimbledon Common, with their ponds, their hawthorn thickets, their paths frequented by nursemaids and children, as exercising ground for a poet.

However resolutely Swinburne tried to make his new residence in Putney seem a matter of choice, really there was no choice left. If he was to live, he could no longer live alone. He had wrecked his health and nearly died through what the Dictionary of National Biography, primly pursing its lips and then opening them just wide enough to permit the useful word to sidle out, calls 'imprudences'. These were brandy, rackety companions, and, at one period, visits to an establishment in St. John's Wood's then dubiously respectable groves, where, in luxurious rooms, a couple of blonde Amazons flagellated the customers who were prepared to pay handsomely for such special pleasures. All his life, Swinburne's far from secret obsession with the idea of pleasure being driven tandem with pain would appear in his early poetry and his two novels, in a few tediously ridiculous verses and dramas he wrote on the subject, and in letters to intimate friends. Even his descriptions of nature are frequently of a force, a mightier Amazon, who is most beautiful when she sends mortals spinning, penetrates them, like ecstatic pagan Saint Sebastians, with her keen silver arrows of rain and wind, and strikes them senseless to the

18

ground. 'I wish I could command storm at will, like a witch', he sighs to his favourite cousin, Mary Gordon Leith. In his novel 'Lesbia Brandon', the rough sea scourges the boy, Herbert Seyton, who gives himself up rapturously to its stinging embraces as young Algernon Swinburne used to do, throwing him back on the beach 'whipped . . . into a single blush of the whole skin'. Long after they settle at The Pines, he describes in a letter to Watts a country ramble from which he gets home so stung and torn by nettles and brambles that he feels happily like a truant schoolboy again, 'returning from a subsequent and consequent interview with the Head Master' back in his days at Eton, where the neurosis began. It was perhaps the requirement of those same implacable, excruciating tensions which made him a great poet, which had ordered him to climb the unclimbed Culver Cliff (and fall fainting at the top), and which set his limbs twitching uncontrollably and his voice shrilling up to a manic scream when he declaimed his poetry. Before his final collapse and withdrawal to Putney, the visits to the house in St. John's Wood had long ceased, so far as his anxious friends could tell, but probably only because he could no longer afford them. The fascination did not diminish.

Swinburne's finances were tottering towards a climax too. He had been harrassed by money difficulties ever since 1866, when his publisher, Edward Moxon, alarmed by the hue and cry of British prudery rushing barking out of its kennel, had withdrawn the first series of 'Poems and Ballads' in fear of public prosecution. A new, luckily far more courageous, but also less reputable publisher was quickly found. John Camden Hotten's list, in which the capture of Swinburne was the biggest triumph, also contained one or two 'curious' items with titles such as 'The Romance of Chastisement; or Revelations of the School or

Bedroom' by 'An Expert', and his financial dealings with his authors were apparently devious. 'The worthy Mr. Hotten', Swinburne wrote reminiscently in 1888, '. . . was a serviceable sort of fellow in his way, but decidedly what Dr. Johnson would have called "a shady lot" and Lord Chesterfield "a rum customer".' According to Hotten, 'Poems and Ballads' only sold three editions, which is decidedly rum when one recalls that all England was reading it, and he appears not to have deemed it necessary to present the poet with a statement of his earnings for three years. In his thirties, as famous and talked about, with scandal and adulation, as Byron had been, Swinburne had depended largely on an allowance, generous for those days, of £200 a year made to him, as though he were still an undergraduate, by his father, Admiral Swinburne. On both sides he came from ancient and aristocratic families—the Swinburnes of Northumberland, the Ashburnhams of Sussex. His mother, Lady Jane Swinburne, was the fourth daughter of the third Earl of Ashburnham.

She and his father knew about the 'fearful propensity' to drink, as she anxiously called it, if not about St. John's Wood. Frequently in those years, the old Admiral, not well and plagued by gout, had to travel to London from Oxfordshire, where the Swinburnes had moved after leaving East Dene, the house at Bonchurch, to take Algernon back to be nursed by his mother and sisters. There were four of them, all younger than he—Alice, Edith (Swinburne's favourite, who died young), Charlotte, and Isabel, a Victorian chime of girls, and at the very end, a brother, Edward, who seemed not to like him much, but loved music passionately and married—disastrously, it turned out—a half-German cousin, Olga Thumann. They ran to affectionate nicknames in the family. The Admiral was Pino, Lady Jane was Mimmie. She had the cultivated accomplishments of her class and had passed some of them on to Algernon—a love for French and Italian literature, for Shakespeare, Dickens and Scott. She always carried with her when she travelled a portfolio of the water-colours of Turner, who has been a friend of her father-in-law's. Swinburne was 'brought up on them.' The girls, Ally, Wibbie, and Abba, were mildly 'talented'. Because of his early religious fervour and beautiful readings aloud from the Bible, Pino and Mimmie had once artlessly hoped that their elder son might enter the Church.

In this pious family circle with its morning prayers, its evening readings aloud, its placid country pursuits, Swinburne would settle down resignedly for months at a time. He adapted to surroundings like a chameleon dropped on a green sofa. Convalescent, cut off from what his adored hero Mazzini called 'the perilous stuff', he would seem happily immersed in his work and reading, until suddenly the lawns of Holmwood, the tap of croquet balls, the consort of cultured female voices all became insufferably boring. He pined for good intellectual male talk, for London.

'There is no one here who can talk about anything which remotely interests me', he complained in a letter to Watts, begging for a long resuscitating one back. Soon he would return to London, and, before long, fresh disquieting rumours would reach Oxfordshire.

Between 1877, when the Admiral died, and 1879, there were periods when Swinburne occasionally dropped out of sight altogether of his friends and family. Prostrate in his lodgings, he sometimes lay for weeks in a stupor, unable to digest food or to hold a pen. When he was well enough to write shaky, belated explanations, he gave his condition polite noms de plume such as 'indigestion' or 'influenza'. Possibly he really believed he had been suffering from these complaints; when sober, he appeared to be able to wipe all

21

inconvenient memories happily out of his mind, and even to shake his head a little, apparently in all sincerity and without batting a sandy eyelash, over insobriety in others. His behaviour at that time was often memorable enough to his embarrassed friends. His hosts, if they were in the know, hid or kept a sharp eye on the liquor. For those who did not, the evening was apt to be punctuated by loud falsetto chanting and Terpsichorean displays, terminating in a sudden thump. Meanwhile the duns gathered at his door, and everything got in a frightful mess. Important letters, manuscripts, agreements, all rose up in the Bloomsbury air like Alice's pack of cards and vanished, and after he struggled out of bed he frequently could not remember anything at all about them. His deafness, a family inheritance, began to trouble him more. In the early spring of 1878, he managed to see the proofs of the second series of 'Poems and Ballads' through the press, but by May he was again so ill (a 'feverish cold in an aggravated form', he wrote to Robert Browning) that he could not accept the invitation of his 'Master', Victor Hugo, to attend a Voltaire festival in Paris at the end of the month. After May, the flood of letters suddenly dries up until September, when he manages to pen an irritable scrawl to Watts. Half dead, weak as a kitten from 'protracted and painful sickness', he has yet noticed 'to my very great inconvenience', that his copies of Victor Hugo's last three books are missing. Mrs. Magill, his housekeeper— the splendid, long-suffering Jane Magill, who faithfully answers all the agitated notes from Swinburne's mother, Lady Jane Swinburne, asking is he well, ill, out of London, for why has he not written?—rather thinks Watts borrowed them, but cannot be sure. In the fearful confusion of Guildford Street things get swallowed up very easily. If so, kindly send back by return of post. And after that, total, ominous silence engulfs the whole dishevelled room, obliterates the mislaid books and their fate, and closes in on their owner for nine months. The next letter from Swinburne is in June 1879, and he is once more back at Holmwood.

This time it was Watts who had saved him, acting as quickly and energetically as the French fishermen had done when they leant over the side of their boat and added him to the day's catch. Swinburne was dying miserably of delirium tremens when Watts fished him out of the depths and removed him to dry land in Putney. There is a story that an acquaintance caught sight of the pair in a four-wheeler, Swinburne lying back in the corner looking ghastly, and was astonished when no notice was taken of his cheerful salutation. It was a day in early June, and a sort of abduction was taking place. The joint household at The Pines was not yet thought of. Swinburne was driven to a house called Ivy Lodge, in Werter Road, Putney, which belonged to Watts' married sister, a Mrs. Mason, and put to bed in the dining-room on the ground floor. We do not know what this lady thought of the sudden invasion of her dining-room by the visitor. Her little boy must be kept quiet. The cook had to be instructed to concoct soups and arrowroots that Swinburne might be tempted to taste. For Watts, at any rate, it was a moment of subdued triumph. He had no legal rights—legality was strongly in his blood—yet he had managed to bring Algernon, who when well was frequently irascible and difficult to control, to Ivy Lodge. Lady Jane Swinburne wrote gratefully to say how thankful she was that her son was out of London (so remote, so rustic did Putney seem in those days). The 'desperate attempt', as Watts called it, had begun.

Walter Theodore Watts had a broad brow, a chin as round and firm as an apple peeping out below a tremendous moustache, and remarkably steady nut-brown eyes. He looked as though he had been born wearing a frock-coat. He

23

was the son of a solicitor in the little town of St. Ives, Huntingdonshire, who was much esteemed locally for his potterings in geology and archaeology, and who made a special study of luminous meteors, and who loved to roam in the cowslip meadows beside the slow-moving glassy Ouse, looking at birds and insects. His mother's family, the Duntons, came from East Anglia. Beneath the frock-coat beat an incurably romantic heart. He had a passion for gypsies. In his boyhood, he had come across the wandering tribes of the Gryengroes, horse-coping Romanies who bought ponies in the Welsh mountains and sold them at the English fairs. He had once seen George Borrow, his hero, swimming at Yarmouth, and when he came to London in 1872 he contrived to meet Borrow, dry and fully clothed, and have a few conversations with him, which he zealously recorded. With his swarthy colouring, he liked to think that he was an honorary Romany himself, and he did not actually deny the doubtful legend that at some time in his youth he might have lived for a while with the Gryengroes.

Studying that calm face, one is struck by something rather doggy about it. Yes, Watts resembles a dependable dog whose appearance would inspire confidence in the most highly strung children—the Darling family's Nana, perhaps, or a benign St. Bernard whose mission in life is the rescue of benighted travellers. He was born to rescue, and to attach himself with quiet tenacity to heroes. George Borrow, glowing with health, had come out of the sea, put on his clothes, and walked briskly away. Besides, when he had persisted in following up that brief early glimpse, a little of Watts' rapture had faded. Borrow, he observed, always carried a gigantic, bulging green umbrella when he went for a country tramp on a dull day. Could he, Watts wondered uneasily, be classed as a real 'Child of the Open Air' when he preferred the shelter of such an umbrella to the feel of

The Pines in 1895 (from a drawing by Herbert Railton reproduced in
the *Illustrated London News*)

Summer at The Pines: Swinburne (above) and Watts-Dunton at the
windows

*Photo: Poole, Putney*

rain pelting on his splendid head? Watts took Nature seriously.

He met Swinburne in London, after he had made the decision that his practice of his father's profession should come second to the literary life. Through his brother Alfred—also a solicitor, who practised in London and was in demand in all sorts of social circles because he was a natural wit, a Yorick who could set the table in a roar while remaining the picture of melancholy himself—he met all the Pre-Raphaelite poets and painters under whose spell he had come when he was still at St. Ives, pondering what to do. Alfred died suddenly, but by now the less showy brother was well established. He turned up everywhere—breakfasting with Whistler; staying with the William Morrises at Kelmscott and going upstairs after dinner with Rossetti to listen to the snoring of young owls somewhere behind the timbers of the ghostly attics; attending Ford Madox Brown's Fitzroy Square evenings where Swinburne, Rossetti, and Morris were the enthroned trinity, round whom clustered lady worshippers dressed in 'a curious antique style of costume *à la bergère*'. They were impressed by Watts. There was something marvellously soothing about his solid shape, his serious, enquiring mind, his doggy readiness to be always on hand to admire or console. He began to write literary criticisms for the weekly journal, the *Examiner*, but he kept on his legal chambers in London until nearly the end of his life. It was as a man of the law, as well as a rising man of letters, that his friends came to value him. None of these quarrelsome, gifted men could really qualify as a genuine Child of the Open Air, perhaps (except little Swinburne, who loved to scamper along with the raindrops glistening in his red curls, and Swinburne, at the start, had snubbed Watts). Yet they were all children, he saw plainly—helpless in business matters, luminous at their easels or writing tables or printing presses, wretchedly fogged by the harsher ways of the world.

Watts had advised Rossetti successfully over a delicate matter of a woman who had forged a cheque in his name. He acted for him and Madox Brown when the Morris firm, which made craftsmen pieces of furniture, stained glass, and metal-work such as later dignified the front door of The Pines, came to an end in bitter divisions of Pre-Raphaelite brotherly feeling. He became the devoted and trusted friend of the last miserable years when Rossetti, bloated and crazy with chloral and whisky, had quarrelled with most of his old friends and trusted practically nobody, even the birds who seemed to be jibing at him, he thought, in the over-grown garden of his house in Cheyne Walk. To Watts, he was the hero of heroes, who would never be replaced, but he was past rescuing. He was to die in Watts' arms in a bungalow at Birchington-on-Sea in 1882.

By then, Watts' slow, singular concentration of purpose had long been turned on Swinburne. Their first meeting was far from promising. He was prepared to admire ardently. The thrilling new music of 'Atalanta' and 'Poems and Ballads', read in the tranquillity of St. Ives, had helped to change his life. It is thought that they met among the mannered shepherdesses at one of Madox Brown's evenings in 1872—perhaps in March, when Swinburne came briefly to London between periods of enforced rustication in Oxfordshire and Scotland, where later that summer he joined one of Benjamin Jowett's reading parties. Better in health, he was not inclined to be less arrogant. Once, at Lord Houghton's house in his youth, he was supposed to have turned his back rudely on Tennyson. When he first met Oscar Wilde, years later, he would say only a couple of cold sentences to him because he knew that Wilde was anxious to meet him. Watts made little impression of any

26

kind. But Swinburne was desperate to leave his publisher, Hotten, and find another home and better terms for his new long drama 'Bothwell'. Hotten refused to release him, and, furthermore, had some shady hold on him in connection with a series of drawings of childishly indecent scenes of schoolboy 'swishings', which one of the publisher's tame artists had been commissioned to execute for his private delectation. After Madox Brown reminded him that the rather ponderous provincial he had barely noticed that evening in Fitzroy Square was a skilled lawyer who understood the muddled affairs of literary men, he applied to Watts for advice (though he kept quiet about the drawings).

Watts gave it with masterly tact and subtlety. He looked beyond the row with Hotten to the future, like a good literary agent. Swinburne must be careful not to let 'Bothwell' go too cheaply. And what about the American market? He had started negotiations on excellent terms with Chapman and Hall, but he warned Swinburne to beware of showing too eagerly that he needed cash, and used a bit of country shrewdness, maybe picked up from the Gryengroes, to point the advice: 'Mr. Chapman is not likely to take a mean advantage (he is a gentleman). But it is wonderful how practical gentlemen are in business matters, as you may have observed if you have ever bought a horse from a friend or sold one to him. Imperceptibly to himself, Mr. Chapman would be more anxious to deal liberally with you if he thought we didn't care a damn whether he dealt with us or not.' Swinburne was impressed, in his turn, by this authoritative voice, so sensible and seemingly selfless, so unlike anything he had heard before. It was true that Hotten hung on grimly and the gentlemanly Mr. Chapman hesitated and stood off. Watts quickly filed a suit against Hotten, but before it came into court the publisher died suddenly. On his new friend's advice, Swinburne decided

27

to remain with Hotten's partner, Andrew Chatto, a man of very different character, who took on the business, expunged the 'curious' items from his list, and continued to publish Swinburne to the end of his life.

The unlikely and almost comic friendship deepened rapidly. Watts was now living close to Swinburne, who at the time had lodgings in Holborn, and they lunched or dined together frequently at nearby eating houses, the Rainbow, or the Cock, or the London. Let us, Swinburne had already suggested, 'begin mutually to drop the Mr. in writing as friends', so it became 'My dear Watts', 'Yours ever A. C. Swinburne', and continued to be so for some years after they settled at The Pines, on the infrequent occasions that they were separated from one another. The easy give and take of Christian names before the first bloom is on, let alone off, an acquaintanceship, was still far away. But with his dear Watts, Swinburne obviously leant back, felt increasingly at ease and even playful—not as he was with Lord Houghton or John Nichol, his old friend from Balliol days, but sufficiently trusting to crack a ribald joke or two and to hymn (unsuccessfully) the works of the 'martyred Marquis' de Sade, to which Houghton had introduced him all those years ago at Fryston. Did he not, he wrote gaily, owe to de Sade, and above all, to *Justine, ou les Malheurs de la Vertu*, 'the means of expressing in some not wholly inadequate degree my sentiments towards God and Man?' Watts, who certainly had heard from Rossetti about the St. John's Wood period of Swinburne's life, replied without enthusiasm. In 1876, he left the *Examiner* and joined the staff of the famous *Athenaeum* as literary critic, and through him, Swinburne became a frequent contributor. His influence was increasing, but he had to proceed carefully and with restraint. He could do nothing to curb the disastrous drinking while Algernon lived alone in his untidy rooms,

28

where his friends could seek him out—Richard Burton, for instance, who turned up now and then from the ends of the earth, and (it was said) had first started Swinburne off on brandy, and had introduced him to the bizarre Cannibal Club, where the Marquis de Sade might have felt quite at home under the horrid emblem of a Negro gnawing at a human thigh bone; or John Nichol, who was now a professor at Glasgow. It was a hard-drinking holiday with Nichol in 1878 that led to Swinburne's final breakdown, to the nine months of his total silence, and then to Werter Road, Putney, where we left him lying in Mrs. Mason's dining-room while the suburban sparrows twittered in the ivy, and little Bertie was forbidden to prance on his wooden horse because of Mr. Swinburne, and the stockpot for the manufacture of nourishing broths that would gently restore a ruined digestion simmered constantly on the kitchen stove.

Watts had removed Swinburne to a place of safety, but what really saved him was his own incredible vitality, which bobbed up indomitably in the face of the doctors who were shaking their heads. In spite of his small frame and girlish sloping shoulders, he had inherited the iron constitution that had made the Swinburnes of Northumberland a hardy, prolific race. An ancestress had given birth to thirty children, and, we are told, 'walked in Newcastle with a mob after her', curious to see this tall and comely prodigy of fecundity. Swinburne's French-born grandfather, Sir John Swinburne of Capheaton Hall, the friend of Mirabeau and John Wilkes, lived to a vigorous ninety-eight, riding and hunting for most of his life, and cheerfully surviving a trepanning operation on his skull after a shooting accident. 'The Swinburnes have a tendency to live', calmly observed his daughter, Julia Swinburne—Swinburne's Aunt Ju, who followed it to the letter by reaching the same age, a chipper old lady, tumbling about in her room but rising a day or two later none the worse, and exhausting mere juveniles of eighty or so by her energy. Swinburne had seemed possessed by a sort of demonic spirit of self-destruction, a Bacchic familiar who had egged him on at intervals over the past years to those 'imprudences' that might well have felled a man like an ox. But his strange little body, with its look of being not quite human, was also inhabited by the tough family talent for triumphing over the physical vicissitudes of thirty children, sawn skulls, old age. In a very few days after his arrival at Ivy Lodge, he was miraculously up and about, even walking on Putney Heath, as though the nightmares and miseries of the last months had been nothing more alarming than one of Aunt Ju's tumbles.

It is probable that he remembered little about them. From Holmwood, where he went later in June, he wrote indignantly to 'my dear Watts' complaining about 'one more of those offensively absurd announcements about my health which would appear to have become a stock-in-trade speciality of the *Athenaeum*', irritably re-named by him the *Assenaeum*. Could Watts somehow contradict it? (The offending paragraph was mild and respectful in the extreme.) As always, when his stomach stopped being queazy and his head cleared and he succeeded in obliterating so wonderfully any unpleasant memories of his latest 'bilious attack' or 'chronic insomnia', the divine, durable gift came flooding back. He was writing hard. He had finished a new poem, 'On the Cliffs', and his book on Shakespeare was 'getting on like a house in flames', and when was Watts coming down so that he might read all to him?

Also there was a great deal to be discussed, though not by Algernon. As his brother Edward remarked, money was 'beyond his ken'. It had been agreed that Swinburne was to set up with Watts 'as a suburban householder', he wrote to John Nichol. His financial ability to do so was the subject of long conferences between his dependable friend Mr. Watts and his relieved mother, who was only too anxious to further 'any plans that may give hope of real good for him'. She could do nothing herself. She was getting old, and he had often told her bluntly that it bored him to death to live at home, yet he could not be allowed to go back to solitary lodgings in London. Furthermore, she had just sold Holmwood and must try to find a new home, on soil that would be better for her rheumatism than the misty Thames Valley, for herself and her daughters. (Edward married that year.) The poor lady must often have felt that her son was a sort of wonderful changeling who had somehow been substituted for the true infant of whom she had been brought to bed one day in April forty-two years ago, in such strangely haphazard fashion, while on a short visit with her husband to a doubtless not greatly pleased relation in Chester Street, Grosvenor Square. Her tender pride in him was immense, but the problem of his future, now that the Admiral was no longer there to travel to London and bring him back, would have been overwhelming if it had not been for his providential friendship with Mr. Watts. Between the business of presiding over the disintegration of a home about to fly off in different directions, tables, chairs, carpets, servants and all—one must decide what furniture to offer for sale to the new owners, what must be stored, and Sotheby's man was coming down to give an opinion on the library, and how heartlessly, indifferently delightful the garden had chosen to look this summer!—Lady Jane held confabulations with Watts. The Admiral had left Algernon £5,000 when he died; his property was divided equally among the five children, with a life interest for Lady Jane. It was finally arranged that Algernon would receive at once a further £2,000, the

31

figure at which his father's valuable books and prints were valued; according to the Admiral's will, he would have inherited it on her death. A further £200 a year would be paid to him for the next four years, but into Watts' banking account. Edward Swinburne, who perhaps felt that Algernon had been treated too handsomely, wrote to Watts, after the guest had returned to Putney, explaining on behalf of his mother that all this business had been settled. At his suggestion, the £2,000 had been split up into two bonds of £1,000 each, 'in case', he observed acidly, 'Algernon should be taken with a paroxysm of extravagance and want suddenly to spend £200 or so on some book; he will now have to sell £1,000 to get hold of £100'. Even though such transactions were beyond his brother's understanding, there was still the danger that 'someone might tell him, if your back was turned, how to do it'.

Watts had been officially appointed custodian. The lease of The Pines was taken out that September for twenty-one years in his name, and he held the purse-strings, but the major share of the purse belonged to Swinburne. It was a constant source of irritation to many of Swinburne's critical pre-Watts friends that later accounts of the joint household (including Max Beerbohm's) often made out that he was merely Watts' guest at The Pines, even a private patient, a sort of ailing Man Who Came to Dinner and was suffered to stay on and on under his host's hospitable roof which could not, as a matter of fact, have existed without him. Watts never, so far as we know, contradicted the impression. He may have come to believe it, as he liked to be indulgent to the legends of his dash of Romany blood and his early days, before the spiritual frock-coat had hardened like shellac over his chest, when, a real Child of the Open Air, he had flirted among the foxgloves and harebells with the pretty little gypsy girls of the prosperous, handsome Gryengroes.

# III

IN OCTOBER, 1880, Lady Jane wrote to Watts from Leigh House, Bradford-on-Avon, the new home where she had settled with Ally, Wibbie and Abba. She wrote with emotion, thanking Algernon's friend for his 'very kind . . . consolitory letter'; the cultured lady's spelling, and occasionally her grammar, went to pieces when her feelings were moved. She has been to The Pines, and 'It is the greatest possible comfort to me to have seen my very dear son so well and happy. The contrast that it was to what I used to see him was something quite beyond words, and I cannot say how thankful I was—nor can I tell you how much I feel your care of him—and I am really quite happy about him.' Here she paused, perhaps, looked out of the window at Wiltshire, and sighed before resuming. 'The return to the religious faith of his youth I feel is so much more hopeful when that fatal tendency from which he has suffered so much is got the better of.'

Mimmie was being too optimistic once again. There was, and is, a church very near The Pines. On Sundays its insistent bells, penetrating his deafness, must have annoyed Swinburne as they summoned the bands of the faithful, dressed in their best, carrying their prayerbooks, from the quiet leafy roads branching out on either side of Putney Hill, but if the Rector called in the hopes of seeing the celebrated new resident, those hopes were certainly dashed. The English Sabbath was a detestable day for

33

Swinburne. By now, even if the Rector did not know him by sight, many of the good people of Putney did. He walked up the Hill every morning, so punctually that matrons peering from behind their lace curtains could set their clocks by him if they chose—every morning, that is, except Sunday. Then Putney Heath was crowded with family parties, with shopkeepers and their girls, with mongrels frisking in the sun and children running over the grass with their kites or hoops. Swinburne, shrinking from the stare of the curious (though few in the Sunday crowds could have known who it was, or would have been much wiser if they had been told, the weird little figure with the cloud of red hair, half-tripping, half-strutting along, must have excited some hearty Cockney guffaws) disciplined himself to mope at home on that day and leave Putney in the dull coils of 'the Galilean serpent'. Some of the other inmates of The Pines certainly took themselves off to church; they did so, one can be sure, with tactful unobtrusiveness. Watts' own beliefs were strong for God in Nature, Nature in God, one and indivisible. The wind from the heath blew fitfully, but he was a conventional Victorian whose roots were firmly planted in a respectable middle-class upbringing. His poems are full of lines such as:

> 'God heard me not', says he, 'Blessed be God!'
> And dies. But as he nears the pearly strand,
> Heav'n's outer coast where waiting angels stand,
> He looks below. 'Farewell, thou hooded clod,
> Brown corpse the vultures tear on bloody sand,'

and so on. Yet he insisted that Swinburne's free thinking must be respected. He knew him too well to risk anything else. Swinburne, inviting a few friends earlier that year to trust themselves to the South Western railway and attend 'my house-and-verse-warming' at The Pines (he was going to give a reading of some new poems), gaily named 'the day known to a few surviving adherents of an execrable superstition as next Wednesday, April 28th, 1880'. 'D. always V.', he nevertheless added ironically to any such plans for the future. For his part, somehow he managed to turn his worst deaf ear to the chanting of Watts' angelic coastguards. The mutually tolerant arrangement worked, but the female members of the household must have sighed with and for Lady Jane.

It is a shock to find that there are females present. From the accounts of Beerbohm and other visitors to The Pines, one pictures a cosy bachelor establishment. There were, of course, the faceless, all but tongueless caps and aprons who carried in the noble leg of mutton; took it out and offered up the apple tart; whitened the steps and polished the bronze door-knocker; refrained from officious dusting of Mr. Swinburne's and Mr. Watts' desks; lugged up enamel cans of hot water and slop-pails and brass scuttles of coals. There were probably, for a house of that size and for its occupants' combined income, two maid-servants. There was that Hetty Priest to whom, decades later, old Watts would leave £50 in his will 'as a small acknowledgement of her services as a domestic to my late dear friend Algernon Charles Swinburne when he first came to live with me, much out of health, more than thirty years ago'. Hetty must have known more about the inner life of The Pines than anybody, but she remains inscrutable, and Swinburne never seemed to see servants, or taste food, or note the look of rooms, or the clothes on people's backs, or show much interest in anything but his poetry and the poetry of others, his library, and the intellectual and political questions and quarrels of the day. Was Hetty, perhaps, the cook in Mrs. Mason's employ at Ivy Lodge who had concocted the beef-teas and jellies when Swinburne was brought there, weak and shattered, in 1879? In the account left by a friend, Coulson Kernaghan, this comic stage domestic emerges triumphantly from her kitchen as though from the wings, brandishing an empty dish which has come out on the distinguished sick-room tray, and crying 'He's a-took it!' Had Hetty moved from Ivy Lodge to The Pines with her mistress?

For Watts' two sisters, Mrs. Charles Mason and Miss Theresa Watts, had come to live there too. (Later, it seems that Miss Watts went away.) There was also the child, Bertie, and it appears that his father, Mr. Charles Mason, was of the household. There are a couple of references to him in Swinburne's correspondence over the first few years at The Pines, and then suddenly he vanishes abruptly without one single speaking line. The enigmatical Mr. Mason ceases, as far as we can tell, to exist. Mrs. Mason and Miss Watts are sufficiently vaporous. Their skirts swish up and down the stairs; they are sometimes present at luncheons and partake of nourishment; they organize such things as the annual painting of the house (the lease specified that The Pines was to be kept in good repair and not to be used for immoral purposes or as a lunatic asylum); they send kind messages to Lady Jane Swinburne and receive them back. Apart from these evidences of vulgar life, they are vapour in female form, and so, one feels, their brother's friend must have viewed them. When they met on the stairs—in such a modest-sized house it was inevitable—Swinburne's greetings, if he noticed them at all, were certainly courteous in the extreme. His manners were always punctilious to women. Yet these ladies, whom he saw every day, were clearly less real to him than his beloved early master, Walter Savage Landor, into whose confused ears he had poured the torrent of his homage when he threw himself at the feet of the old poet in Florence in 1864, on the second of his two visits to Italy. ('So totally am I exhausted that I can hardly hold my pen to express my vexation that I shall be unable to converse with you again', Mr. Landor had written hastily to his young visitor following the trying meeting.) They were far less real than his revered 'Master of Masters', Victor Hugo, whom he had not yet seen in the flesh at all. They seem to have been invisible to others, too. When visitors came to The Pines and recorded their impressions, Mrs. Mason and Miss Watts do not often appear to have been present. It is to be assumed that these self-effacing women ate off trays in their bedrooms. One can only conjecture how the whole odd party fitted into The Pines. Swinburne was given the best room on the first floor, looking down into the garden, for his library; Watts' study, from Beerbohm's account and others, adjoined the dining-room. Hetty and her colleague must have slept below in the dark basement where the bells hung on jangling wires high along the passage wall, black beetles came out at night from under the dresser, the range squatted like a sullen blackamoor who would roar when the dampers were pulled out in the morning, and Dido, the woolly house-dog, whined and chased the Putney urchins and rats in her sleep.

For Swinburne, the change to The Pines was a transformation so absolute, so extraordinary as to amount to being born again. He says so in his poetry. In his birthday month of April, 1882, nearly three years after his departure to Putney, he sat down and wrote the verses gratefully dedicating 'Tristram of Lyonesse' to Watts, 'My best friend'.

Life stands crowned
Here with the best one thing it ever found
As of my soul's best birthdays dawns the third.

The contrast, as Mimmie observed, was something quite beyond words. He was completely restored to health and, like a three-year-old child, he had learned his way round a whole new world. Since coming down rather abruptly and ingloriously from Oxford, he had lived alone when he was not rusticated in the family home. There had been a time when he and George Meredith had lodged with Gabriel Rossetti in Tudor House, the rambling old Chelsea mansion that was part of a larger vanished house which had belonged to Queen Katherine Parr. It had not been a success. Even when he was lonely and ill, he had preferred freedom in which to work and read; to come and go and get drunk with whatever friends he pleased; to pirouette and declaim hymns in praise of liberty for Italy and for all men; to lie naked of a summer's day on his bed in his lodgings, as he appears in George Moore's famous description of paying a disconcerting call on him, like a weird, wilting tulip with an outsize red head on a thin white stalk. His spirits galloped in those days, before weariness and melancholy set in, and one can hear them galloping in the letters he dashed off to his friends in the bold, staggering script that he was pleased to fancy was not unlike the calligraphy of de Sade. He loved to amuse the most favoured with wild obscene or profane nonsense and brilliantly funny parodies. Meredith and the others roared with laughter over the burlesque French novel, *La Fille du policeman*, in which the Bishop of Londres rapes the heroine in a cab and Prince Albert misbehaves atrociously. All the same, Gabriel Rossetti had paternally warned him, not long before the painful, never-to-be-explained moment when this dearest of all Swinburne's friends suddenly refused to see him any more, that 'every line he (Swinburne) had ever written' would one day certainly be 'religiously raked up' by scribblers yet unborn, peeping and botanizing for the meanest weed on the graves

38

of the great. Some of their circle might not have had the heart or the good sense to burn 'these wonderfully funny things' with which he regaled them. Rossetti was right, of course. Numbers of their recipients carefully kept them (Edward Burne-Jones treasured his until 1890, when he destroyed them regretfully, feeling that if he did not, he wrote to his wife, 'Swinburne's ghost would pursue mine through the next world'), and some of the letters were dynamite later on. But Swinburne had replied with a splendid characteristic flash of spirit: 'As to privacy, if we are to be shackled in our inmost intercourse with our closest friends by the fear of future vermin, we may as well resign all liberty, and all thought of elbow-room for fun and confidence of any kind, at once.'

All his life, in his lordly Swinburne fashion, he had been used to plenty of elbow-room, literally. His native background was the aristocratic one of large houses surrounded by deep old lawns and ancient trees in the leaves of which a whole nestful of children could hide and call to each other, within sight or reach of the sea and of wild country over which he and his cousins had galloped their ponies. The ultimate luxury of the well-off—the ability to avoid one's nearest and dearest at will—had been his whenever he cared to return to it. Now here he was wedged in a rather small middle-class home in Putney filled to capacity with people who, with the exception of Watts, spoke a different language. He had brightened up, soon after they all moved into The Pines, at the sight of little Bertie Mason. Swinburne had always been fond of children. He wrote to Mimmie describing how the little boy had behaved badly at lunch, and how he had bought him a box of preserved fruits from Fortnum and Mason. Watts had early on dropped tactful hints to his friend about his own behaviour under the new circumstances. Swinburne's language was frequently as colourful and fluent as a London cabbie's. His flights of abuse of somebody who had angered him were always vehement. Edmund Gosse, years later, remembered a fairly temperate verbal bludgeoning of one such unfortunate. 'He had better be careful', it ran, 'If I am obliged (*very slowly*) to take the cudgel in my hand, (*rapid exultation*) the rafters of the hovel where he skulks and sniggers shall ring with the loudest whacks ever administered in discipline or chastisement to a howling churl.' Now, Watts suggested, if he must break out and swear in mixed company at The Pines, would he do so in French? He could let himself go equally picturesquely in Gallic invective. There must be no more lying about naked on the bed at The Pines, of course. A cap and apron might come along with a can of hot water, or one of the Watts ladies, going upstairs to remove a bonnet, might glance through a half-open door, and—'*Oh monsieur, quelles horreurs!*' as Swinburne was fond of making the unfortunate heroine exclaim piteously in his frequent parodying allusions to *Justine, ou les Malheurs de la Vertu* for the amusement of Lord Houghton and other favoured correspondents.

Swinburne adapted himself with wonderful docility. The nagging problem which for so long had plagued all the people who were truly fond of him had been solved. Ruskin had helplessly summed it up fourteen years earlier, just as 'Poems and Ballads' was about to burst marvellously on the world to be fulminated against in pulpits and chanted rapturously through college quads, as the impossibility of knowing 'what to do with and for' Algernon. Ruskin told Swinburne that he would as soon fault him or his poems as he would blame a thundercloud or a nightshade blossom for being 'wonderful and beautiful', but 'dreadful and deadly' too. Yet what to do with this oppressive purple patch of vapour, this exquisite poisonous and self-poisoning plant except watch them taking their natural course? Ruskin sensibly thought that the *'one* thing' anybody could therapeutically do to help Swinburne was 'to soothe him and trust in him', though for himself, he added, 'I am afraid only of his dying'.

This sage council was, as it turned out, the course successfully followed by Watts. He knew that he must seem to 'trust' Swinburne and somehow manage to supply the steady surveillance of every aspect of his friend's life that was to last until death. But to soothe—ah yes, that was where the extraordinary man, with his bright eyes, his capacious brow, his air of being a good listener to the litigious tangles of anxious clients, came out strongly. He must have been extraordinary to make men as different and difficult as Rossetti, Swinburne, and Tennyson all repose their confidence in him as though thankfully depositing valuables in a reliable strong-box. And he was better than that. He paid an interest on the contents that was somehow enriching to men more splendidly dowered than himself. It must be admitted that his charm does not always show itself in his writing, if one searches the files of the *Examiner* or the *Athenaeum*. Time has not lain lightly on his style. His conversation was much admired by many, and one remembers the witty brother Alfred who died, but the voice of Walter (Swinburne, when they eventually took the enormous plunge into Christian names after ten years of living in each other's pockets at The Pines, always called him by his first name, not by the 'Theodore' of Beerbohm's recollection) appears to be more serious and to make its effect with a relentless flow of anecdotage. He had a sense of fun but no wit. Yet the destroyed face of Gabriel Rossetti would brighten wonderfully, his brother William records, when Watts came into the room. Rossetti continued to need him right up to the last, after he had long cut himself off from Swinburne and other old friends. In 1881 and 1882, Swinburne had frequently to be left in the care of Mrs. Mason and Miss Watts on the occasions when Watts rushed off to the bedside of the dying Gabriel, the first and most dearly loved of his heroes; a bedroom in Rossetti's house was always kept ready for him. Then we see him later on paying visits to the Tennysons at Aldworth, a house on another noble down in Sussex. The Laureate takes Watts off into a summer-house and reads him his new drama, 'Becket', asking eagerly for his friend's opinion. We may be sure that he got it, at great length, and that it was laudatory. Let us now praise famous men. Early on, the thoughtful solicitor from St. Ives had realized the simple truth that famous men of letters, and poets more than most, need praise pressed down and running over. It is mother's milk to their sensitive muse who may turn pale, droop, and in some cases develop queer symptoms of bile and colic without it. To Ruskin's practical formula for saving Algernon he added the verb 'to admire'. The Pines is to be a summer-house, and a winter-house too, where Swinburne sits contentedly perched—still recognizably like Beerbohm's drawings of the fire-bird Algernon, though begining to lose a few feathers from his flaming topknot, and, with the quiet Putney nights and the regular meals from Hetty's department, developing a stouter breast—warbling a new lyric, or ode, or roundel into Watts' receptive ear and receiving back a generous dipper of the milk of paradise.

> There is a friend that as the wise man saith
> Cleaves closer than a brother; nor to me
> Hath time not shown, through days like waves at strife,
> This truth more sure than all things else but death,
> This pearl most perfect found in all the sea. . .

Thus Swinburne praised Watts in return with warm

42

affection in his dedication of '*your* Tristram'. He had been haunted by the legend since Oxford, when he had written a curious Pre-Raphaelite ballad on it. He had started a new poem on the theme in 1868, but he had mislaid the manuscript, probably in a cab. All his life he lost things; books and papers hid themselves maliciously so that he could not find them, and in 'the paper-heaps of Putneydom' their ingenuity was to increase. Then he had been ill, and 'London . . . or (worse) society', whether of friends or of the Amazons of St. John's Wood, were 'awful clogs on poetry'. But now, hastening over Putney Heath among the nursemaids, returning to the domestic villa and the smell of roasting mutton and the quiet hours of work after the little reviving nap, he had no clogs. The joys and torments of passionate, guilty love poured out of him so ardently that Watts took fright and begged him to tone things down a bit. Might not some of the erotic passages in what Swinburne cheerily described as 'my modest effort to paint a scene of unpretending enjoyment by moonlight' renew all the bedlam of outraged virtue that 'Poems and Ballads' had let loose?

Watts had already insisted that the alarmingly perceptive take-off of the manner and the deep pessimism of the man, Algernon Charles Swinburne, 'Poeta Loquitor', should be omitted from his superb collection of parodies of Tennyson, Browning, Mrs. Browning and others, 'Specimens of Modern Poets: The Heptalogia', which had appeared in 1880. The pin transfixing that particular specimen was inserted, Watts considered, with really too diabolical a twist of melancholy self-knowledge.

> In a maze of monotonous murmur
> Where reason roves ruined by rhyme,
> In a voice neither graver nor firmer
> Than the bells on a fool's cap chime. . .

And then on to worse:

> Some singers indulging in curses
> Though sinful have splendidly sinned;
> But my would-be maleficent verses
> Are nothing but wind.

Could one imagine Tennyson writing anything like that? *Quelles horreurs*, indeed! Swinburne's readiness to laugh at himself was always endearing, but sometimes Watts, with his new, anxious proprietorship, found it excessive. 'Poeta Loquitor' did not get into print until 1918, though the more subtle and even more ruthless 'Nephelidia'—'From the depth of the dreamy decline of the dawn through a notable nimbus of nebulous noonshine / Pallid and pink as the palm of the flag-flower that flickers with fear of the flies as they float'—was included with the rest of the victims in 'The Heptalogia'.

The gratifying dedication of 'Tristram of Lyonesse', which some of Swinburne's sceptical friends read with mixed feelings, was not exaggerated. For the pearl most perfect found in all the sea had somehow managed to bring off what they had all failed to do or had funked trying for Swinburne. He stopped drinking. We do not know for certain what methods Watts used to cure a chronic alcoholic who had been one for fifteen years, off and on, but we would like to know. The favourite legend is that he devised a solemn charade which surely would not have fooled a child to keep away from the chocolate drawer and settle for one fruit-drop a day, yet Swinburne, the story runs, accepted it with alacrity. Something about his drinking had been childish make-believe all along—the clutching of the nearest available decanter, as a drowning man might seize hold of a spar, as Edmund Gosse recalled in the confidential notes he made later to fill in some of the careful blanks in his 'Life of Swinburne'; the fierce swigging of the wine in a sort of gurgling frenzy; the boasting to Sir Charles Dilke that the best way to settle a glass of green chartreuse was to throw two glasses of yellow chartreuse down quick sharp after it. He drank largely through the eye; if the 'perilous stuff' was not there, he seemed not to crave it. So perhaps it is not quite out of character that Watts was said to have reminded him, whose tipple was brandy, that Tennyson always drank port. Curiously enough, he had just been given a few bottles of excellent port on which he would be glad to have Swinburne's opinion. Then, after a week or so of judicious Tennysonian sipping, ought they not to make a change and drink with their meals a little of the glorious wines of Swinburne's 'well-beloved' France? And finally, like an unbelievable wine-waiter skilfully directing the diner's hesitant finger from the most expensive to the cheapest item on the list, Watts spoke enthusiastically of 'Shakespeare's nut-brown October', good old English ale. It has a ring of truth. His utterances, if one can judge from his prose, were doggedly literary. The little bottle of Bass had arrived at Swinburne's place in the dining-room of The Pines, and it remained there for life. E. V. Lucas, a less affectionate observer than Beerbohm, who also made the pilgrimage to the shrine in the nineties, remembered the Bard marching out of the room after the meal (it was dinner) was over, still firmly clasping to his bosom the bottle 'in which a few precious drops remained'. The vine leaves are out of his hair. Now he wears patriotically in that dwindling aureole the green tendrils of the Kentish hop.

There was one last worry for his ingenious friend. Would Swinburne manage to get 'the stuff' when he went out for his walks and smuggle it home to The Pines? So among the rules of behaviour that Watts laid down, or tactfully suggested soon after they joined forces, was a veto on the public houses of Putney. It would be unbecoming if Mr. Swinburne were seen to enter one. Mr. Swinburne agreed. He gave his word, which Watts knew could be relied upon absolutely. But one of the many beings inhabiting that skipping fairy body was a joker. He enjoyed pulling Watts' leg. In a letter a few years later on one of their occasional separations, he says that he is writing an article on Victor Hugo's *La Légende des Siècles* for the *Fortnightly Review*, and that the effort of trying to do justice to his 'Master of Masters' is making his brain boil and his ears buzz. '. . . O how much harder work is conscientious reviewing than original production! I wonder how you keep alive and sane. But Nature, my very dear Sir, has bestowed upon some favoured sons a combination of the loftiest energies by whose means etc. . . .' The acute ear is parodying Mr. Pecksniff, but there may also be a wicked hint of the stately cadences of Nature's permanent member of the fraternity of the open road. Watts' prose style was rather like that. The Darling children were not afraid to romp with Nana even when she kept on after them with gruff barks of warning. So Swinburne teased his watch-dog by walking every morning up the Hill and along Wimbledon Common to the Rose and Crown, two miles away, which is over the Putney border into Wimbledon. There he refreshed himself with a glass of beer—he kept to that, for Nana had an air of authority difficult to push against—before racing home to luncheon, to bow to Miss Watts, another bow to Mrs. Mason, another beer, a benign exchange with Bertie, who was making naughty zoological noises again (it was so wonderful, Swinburne wrote to Mimmie, to feel that there was a child in the house), and then upstairs to his own domain. The compact with Watts had been kept to the letter. The landlord of the Rose and Crown was appreciative of the honour that had been paid to his house. Mr. Swinburne had his own corner,

his own chair in which he sat reading the papers he had
bought at Putney railway station. His great domed head was
a store-house filled with an immense array of English,
French, and Italian literature, of Greek and Latin, stowed
away in the perfect order that eluded his possessions in
life. He seemed to have read everything, and he remembered everything; his letters gave his friends a lively
paper-chase along a trail of quotations and allusions. Yet he
read the papers and the magazines too. Beerbohm, twenty
years later, found it comic that there should be room in the
fabulous store-house for 'our twaddle'. Nobody in the Rose
and Crown paid any attention to the customer in the corner,
unless the landlord proudly but discreetly pointed him out
to favoured newcomers. 'Lord!' said a candid drinker in
astonishment one day, 'He looks as though he hadn't two
ideas to bless himself with.'

The friends who felt with resentment that Watts had
carried Swinburne off in his teeth to bury him jealously in
the obscurity of Putney were wrong in transferring their
own emotions of loss to the abductee. He seemed to be
conscious of no loss at all in the early days at The Pines. The
idea of the academic retreat from which he and Watts could
sally out at will was not entirely wrong, for the first years.
They saw people, and people came to see them. There is no
reason to suppose that Swinburne did not mean exactly
what he wrote in the 'Tristram' dedication. His new life
was standing crowned with the best one thing it ever found,
for had the old one been so happy? In 1876, he had written
wearily to Churton Collins, the critic and literary historian
whom he had met through Jowett at Balliol, of 'the rather
dull monotonous puppet-show of my life which often strikes
me as too barren of action or enjoyment to be much worth
holding to, better than nothingness, or at least seeming
better for a moment'. It is the overriding death-wish of his

beloved Elizabethan dramatists, the deep-rooted desire to shrug off mortality and expose the rotting carcass under the bright robe. Now he was happier, it is clear enough, than he had been since his childhood at East Dene, thanks to Watts. Like Philoctetes, the Greek warrior into whose possession had passed from the dying Hercules a divine bow, the gift of Apollo, which could not miss its mark, but who had received an infection from a serpent's bite so virulent and revolting to others that he was forced to nurse it in wretched isolation, he owed his liberation to a man who was solicitous of the marvellous bow yet not too squeamish to come close to its owner. 'Deplorable and disgusting beyond words.' So Edmund Gosse described Swinburne's state at the time Watts removed him to Putney, in the famous confidential essay that, after much soul-searching, he wrote in 1917 as a dutiful historical postscript to what some among the few survivors who had known the poet, and the many who had heard the legends, felt to be the too tactful, mealy-mouthed omissions in the 'Life'. Addressed to Posterity, and directed to that patiently waiting, bright-eyed lady care of the classical *poste restante* of the British Museum archives, it revealed in cautious, measured terms that his dear friend had worn, for a matter of fifteen years or so, the mingled garland of vine leaves and birch twigs of a chronic drunkard and sexual masochist. It was first published as an Appendix to the Yale University Press edition of the Swinburne Letters in 1962. Gosse admitted and deplored. He constantly and far more bitterly lamented (though not in print) what was to happen to Apollo's bow when it was hung up over the umbrella stand in the stuffy hall at The Pines. Yet, for all his intimate devotion to Swinburne, 'deplorable' and 'disgusting' seem to tiptoe uneasily away from the nasty cave in Guildford Street, holding their noses. Swinburne had no illusions as to which of his friends had been staunch enough to march right in. Watts' middle-aged form seems a droll comparison with the boy Neoptolemus who, in Sophocles' drama, saves the invalid and preserves the gift of the god, but he appeared to have succeeded in doing both, and Gosse never forgave him.

## IV

THE INTERIOR of The Pines was like a rich dark cake stuffed with Pre-Raphaelite fruit, though not all the plums were from the best tree. The same Putney photographer who came one summer day and took the picture of Swinburne and Watts sitting on their hard chairs communing among the daisies has left us photographs, equally evocative, of corners of the house that Watts permitted to be revealed to the curious world during his and his friend's lifetime. It was the only communication The Pines had with the public. Any prose description of what went on behind the celebrated front door was strictly vetoed. A fervently admiring young Irish friend of Watts', James Douglas, wrote a study of his life and work which approaches the subject on tiptoe bearing extravagant sheaves of tribute, but Watts warned him, kindly but firmly, that he must keep off anything personal about the double establishment. He must not even try to describe Watts' appearance. They were hard rules for a would-be biographer, but Douglas had grumblingly to agree. It seems that a brash American female journalist from California who called herself 'Olive Harper' (her real name was Mrs. Helen D'Apery) had once written a totally fictitious 'interview' with Swinburne, although she had never so much as laid eyes on him, which appeared in some Western newspapers. Since then all scribblers were taboo. One could not, of course, do anything about the vulgar fellows who often accepted an invitation to The Pines, shouted respectfully into the great man's ear, turned their beady eyes this way and that while they broke the sacred bread of hospitality and drank the Putney water, and then hurried home to jot down their malicious impressions of the household. Those who asked permission to write a little something about the home life of Mr. Swinburne received from Mr. Watts a loud bark warning them to run for their lives towards the South-Western Railway Station.

But the photographer, Mr. Poole, was allowed to come along one day and set up his tripod, disappear under the cloth, and turn the sharp recording eye of the camera upon the clutter of wonderful objects that, as the years passed, adhered to the surface of The Pines as a collection of strange shells is affixed with glue in elaborate encrustation upon a Victorian work-box. Set fast in the emulsion of an era, these possessions have an air of abiding forever, of sticking together even though the waters of the earth should roll down Putney Hill. They make a pattern of purl upon plain, of whorl upon smooth, of gilding and ornament upon everything, so that I hardly know where to look first, and would have been somewhat at a loss, if the occasion had ever arisen, to decide where it would be safest to sit. Should it be on one of those extraordinary fretted wooden chairs that have a curiously exotic African air, as of the thrones of tribal chiefs? Would I dare to lower myself onto the Chinese day-bed, which emerges like a modern fold-up divan from the jaws of a sort of Oriental booth somewhat resembling a fantastic telephone-box? One name is shouted above all others through the rooms into which we are able to take brief glutted glances, and it is not the name of Swinburne. Like Tennyson's leader wild swan up among the stars in 'The Princess' who clanged the name of Ida, The Pines sang continually of Dante Gabriel, the dearest-loved lost friend of both its masters.

Soon after the move to Putney, Watts had gone back across the river to Chelsea to spend the night with his other sacred charge, the too palpably doomed Rossetti, who could not be rescued, whose black melancholy would never be sent packing by regular meals and a few pleasing literary theories about the superiority of beer to whisky. Next day, returning to Putney after looking in on Whistler—Watts was a sociable man, and we should be wrong to think that only Swinburne was deprived of something in the seclusion of The Pines—he found a waggon standing at the gate. It was loaded with furniture that Rossetti had chosen out of Tudor House and sent to Watts in Putney without saying a word the night before; he enjoyed giving agreeable surprises to his friends. So here stands the splendid lacquer cabinet which he had bought from a hard-up artist friend, George Chapman, who had bought it from a sea-captain home from years of flogging up and down the China Coast, who had bought it from a Frenchman, who said he had looted it from the Imperial Palace. Here are the carved mirrors decorated by Treffry Dunn, Rossetti's Cornish studio assistant, with copies of the Master's lost frescoes showing the Quest for the Holy Grail. They had been painted and had perished on the damp rejecting walls of the Oxford Union long ago when Swinburne, an undergraduate at Balliol, first met him and the younger spirits of the Brotherhood, when it was all roars of laughter and outrageous talk, 'Blue summer then, and always morning and the air sweet and full of bells', as Edward Burne-Jones nostalgically remembered years later. Somewhere in the indigestible fruit-cake is embedded a painted cupboard on which Swinburne—seeming the red-haired, green-eyed, goitrous brother of the Pre-Raphaelite maidens—was the model for St. George. An absurd gilded snake rears up from a pedestal, balancing on the tip of its nose what looks like a Victorian gas-lamp to illuminate the walls, crowded with pictures in heavy frames. 'My girls', Watts skittishly called the gallery of Rossetti crayon drawings of women, and they are stunners to a girl. Some of them stun with the abundance of flesh, the tiger-lily warmth and sensuality of Fanny Schott, whom Rossetti playfully named 'the Elephant'. The loveliest of all is dark haired Janey Morris, the wife of William Morris, for whom Gabriel significantly invented no funny name, who had inhabited his dream more lastingly, more hauntingly, than either coarse 'Elephant' or poor, ethereal 'Guggum', his dead wife, Lizzie Siddal, for whose memory Swinburne had such chivalrous devotion all his life. She lies back moodily on a sofa, stretching out the full length of her long neck like a swan, the leader wild swan herself. And mixed in with Watts' girls are some bad paintings, artist not stated, of his very own ladies, the gypsy damsels, Sinfi Lovell (whom George Meredith admired so much) and Rhona Boswell, creations of the strange man's romantic obsession with the Romanys in his once widely read, now completely forgotten novel 'Aylwin' and the long poem of his later years, 'The Coming of Love'. This is to be the shrine in which Apollo's wondrous bow is hung up and tended with devotion, but most of the other trophies on its walls seem to have been nailed there by Watts to remind visitors that he, too, has made the pilgrimage to Delphi.

Rossetti was now dead. He had died, with Watts beside him, in the Birchington-on-Sea bungalow without ever asking to see Swinburne again. The numerous reminders of Gabriel so piously preserved in The Pines were also reminders of the pain of the inexplicable rejection. Swinburne, sitting in his study looking down at the little Vatican Venus, modestly clutching her drapery, who had translated herself from Cheyne Walk to Putney Hill, still wrote calmly and admiringly of 'poor Gabriel' and his poetry to Rossetti's more solid, less star-touched brother, William. Because of a temperament that was almost awesomely well-balanced, William contrived to remain a staunch friend for life. But to Watts, the receptive ever-ready ear from which there were now, one guesses, no secrets kept, Swinburne let himself go with uninhibited virulence in a letter written in 1882 from his mother's house, where he was staying for a visit of several weeks.

Every year he was sent off by himself for one or two changes of air to Wiltshire. With Mimmie and his sisters on guard, Bradford-on-Avon was judged to be 'safe'. Safety was still not taken for granted, and it would be a matter of extraordinary uneasiness for many more years to come. Except for these regular returns to the family, the only unaccompanied visit Watts allowed Swinburne to make was a short one the following year to his old friend, Benjamin Jowett, the Master of Balliol, in whose household the clashing of cymbals was improbable. Three years after the move to The Pines and the unbelievable victory for the quiet life and modest rations of Shakespeare's nut-brown October, neither Watts nor Lady Jane appeared to feel entirely confident. At the end of that autumn stay at Leigh House in 1882 there was, for instance, a ludicrous family panic over a mistake in the time of the slow train to Paddington, which was the only one on which it was deemed prudent for Algernon, aged forty-five, to travel. The normal thing was to alight at a junction further up the line and board another, faster train to London. But a change meant a wait, and might he not (this seems to be the unvoiced fear in poor Lady Jane's mind) wander into the station refreshment room, suddenly see a brandy bottle, and succumb to the 'fearful propensity' again? Everything is carefully thought out. Algernon will have a nice nourishing lunch first, before driving with his sister Charlotte to be put on the dependable slow, off which Watts will pluck him intact, cheerful, and vertical at Paddington. But the slow is not dependable; it has decided, unknown to the Leigh House family, to gallivant giddily along ten minutes ahead of its usual time. So Algernon has to wait, as patiently as may be, for the next direct dawdler, while Miss Charlotte frantically telegraphs Watts, care of the Paddington station-master, to warn him that Mr. Swinburne will be arriving two hours later than had been settled. When she gets back to Leigh House with the dismal tale, Lady Jane dashes off an agitated note to Watts, hoping that Algernon 'may get home all safe' and apologizing for the anxiety her son's friend must have felt when he met the hitherto reliable slow and found no little red-haired figure among the travellers. Yet Algernon appeared such a wonderfully changed man that 'I do think we may trust him', she writes falteringly, without perceiving that the whole comic business showed how thoroughly they did not.

When Swinburne was away on these lengthy Victorian visits, Watts faithfully forwarded the weekly reviews to alleviate the country boredom. The punctual delivery of shot rubbish, as Swinburne put it, was an event in days even quieter than those at The Pines. Though his bed in Putney might be empty, a constant flow of lordly Swinburnian commands for missing periodicals, urgently needed books, garments which 'the servants' (an imposing retinue seems to be indicated) had omitted to pack, rattled through the letter-box. 'You have sent me the *Academy* for July 3rd, which I did not want—not that for the 10th, which I do.' 'Please send me at once some *stockings* . . . also short of handkerchiefs... also (carefully packed up) the four volumes of the Légende des Siècles, the *second* volume of the Contemplations.' 'I want a change of linen! . . . I awoke without a shirt to my back.' 'Please remember my nail-pincers, etc.' Mrs. Mason must have been permanently busy with brown paper and string.

It was in the *Academy*, during his October rustication, that Swinburne read a notice of Hall Caine's 'Recollections of Dante Gabriel Rossetti'. Caine had been the youthful prop and stay, along with Watts, of Gabriel's last days; it would hardly have prepossessed Swinburne in his favour. And now, he read, Caine appeared to have asserted that the shock of Robert Buchanan's famous attack in 1871 on 'The Fleshly School of Poetry', in particular the poetry and morals of Rossetti and Swinburne, had been as catastrophic in its effect on Gabriel's sanity as the tragic death by an overdose of laudanum of his wife nine years before. To speak of the two events in the same breath seemed insupportable to Swinburne. Could it really be possible that Gabriel had suffered as much torment of mind from the abuse of that 'small piece of dung', Buchanan, as from the terrible loss of 'dear Lizzie', the poor, bright, playful 'Guggum'? For himself, had he not cheerfully ignored Buchanan and far more infamous slinging of mud? After the publication of 'Poems and Ballads', anonymous letters of fanatical violence had pelted in on him along with the praise. A nameless Irish sporting gentleman had threatened to waylay him one night, slip a bag over his head, and castrate him, 'as he had seen his gamekeeper do with cats'. A clergyman had thundered at a Church Congress in Nottingham, more recently still, that while Renan with treacherous praise betrayed Christ, Swinburne insulted Him as He hung on the bitter Cross. The last charge had delighted Swinburne, who took it as a compliment. But he had never lost an hour's sleep, he boasted, over attacks from any quarter.

It was Caine's confident bracketing of 'Guggum's' pathetic slipping out of life and a scribbler's malice as the

56

Swinburne, aged 65

Watts-Dunton

double eclipse of Gabriel's sun which brought the pain and the jealousy tumbling out in a contemptuous letter to Gabriel's devoted friend in Putney. The insult to Lizzie was odious. For women such as Lizzie and Gabriel's holy sister Christina, Swinburne reserved a peculiar tenderness. There were the blonde Amazons, the implacable ones in the vanished grove of the punishing goddess in St. John's Wood, and there were the Lizzies, to whom he behaved as though he were still the model for the young, valiant St. George. The bewilderingly complicated storehouse under that vast dome of skull included compartments for shot rubbish as well as for genius, for violence and for gentleness. Looking at photographs of the splendid brow and the 'eyes of a god', as Max described them, and marking the sudden sloping away of such grandeur into the weak chin and long exposed neck, one fancies that the upper half of the face wrote 'Atalanta' and 'Hertha'. The chin composed the feeble and pathetic flagellant fantasies, such as 'The School-boy's Tragedy, A Lyrical Drama in five acts', which appeared to have been written, as Sir Edmund Gosse disapprovingly stated in a further note forwarded to Posterity care of the British Museum in 1920, in the quiet study at The Pines when all (or nearly all, for somehow one is certain that nothing escaped Watts' X-ray eye) had concluded that Swinburne's taste for the thought of physical pain was as dead as his taste for brandy. But this was not so. Even in the peaceful surburban grove of the Vatican Venus, after nearly twenty years ('The Schoolboy's Tragedy' was written about 1893) of living in the bosom of a sort of ready-made Darling family, with Nana tirelessly on guard to keep the other Lost Boys away, he never truly grew up in the lower, or chin-ward half of his nature; the solitary haunting visions continued to float in through the nursery bars on the window. Gosse states that he and his friend, Thomas J.

57

Wise, the enthusiastic collector and, as it turned out (but the celebrated piece of bibliographic detective work by John Carter and Graham Pollard which unmasked him was made in 1934, when the trusting Gosse was dead), unscrupulous forger of Swinburnian and other items, carefully destroyed this particular 'curiosity'.

The ferocious comment sent to Watts from Leigh House in 1882 seemed to have been penned partly out of protective brother-sister love for Lizzie, partly from Swinburne's brooding sense of loss and unhappiness over the shattering withdrawal of Rossetti's friendship, for no reason, he had told William Rossetti after Gabriel died in the spring, that he had ever been able to imagine. If Caine were right in saying that Buchanan's attack had been as terrible to Gabriel as Lizzie's suicide, then he had been miserably mistaken in his man. 'In that case', he burst out to Watts, 'remembering the loyal, devoted, and unselfish affection which I lavished for fifteen years on the meanest, poorest, most abject and unmanly nature of which any record remains in even literary history, I cannot say I wonder at the final upshot of our relations'. He added (without remembering to substitute his more customary 'Thank Something'), 'Thank God for the difference between my "best friend" of the past and my best friend of the present.'

There already seems to be a difference, we have to note, between the Swinburne who was Gabriel's loyal, devoted, and affectionate friend and the Swinburne who dedicated 'Tristram' to Watts. The fine high spirit of that rejoinder to Rossetti long ago, refusing to condescend to moderate the bubbling flow of funny indecencies in his letters for fear of what 'future vermin' might think of them, appears to be far away. What people are thinking now, what vermin are up to at the present moment, have suddenly become more important. The atmosphere of The Pines, with its variety of tasteful dodges in the way of thick hangings, table covers, antimacassars, for muffling unpleasant currents of cold air, softening sharp furniture edges which might deal one a nasty hack on the shin, and foiling stains of horrid dirty hair-oil, was one of prudence above all things. Something aristocratic has been lost on the cab drive to Putney. For now Swinburne, the brilliant mimic, seems to us to be giving an excellent imitation of a woman, a Madame Swann, who has made a respectable alliance and is anxious to drop unwelcome acquaintances from the past. Or do we catch a faint echo of the priggish Prince Hal, breaking Falstaff's heart and walking on towards the Abbey and so to Agincourt?

Soon after he and Watts settled at The Pines, Swinburne wrote to Edmund Gosse, striking the mingled chord of wounded virtue and sorrow which comes so strangely from him, to deplore the behaviour of one of his old disreputable companions. This was Charles Augustus Howell, a fascinating hanger-on to Pre-Raphaelite circles, an adventurer who lived by his considerable wits and sailed as near the wind as he could without getting himself blown below decks into irons. He had once been Swinburne's confidant in every sadique adventure and fantasy. Swinburne had entreated humbly for Howell's company in letters which this particular vermin, one could be sure, had never tossed lightly into the fire. Now disturbing word had filtered through to Putney that Howell was 'amusing mixed companies of total strangers', Swinburne raged to Gosse, 'by obscene false anecdotes about my private eccentricities of indecent indulgence'. *Mixed* companies of total *strangers*—in some comic way he was as angry over the fact that there were ladies present, and that the audiences were unknown to him, as over the untruth (or otherwise) of the stories. Swinburne was always the pink of old-fashioned politeness with women;

he hoped he would never, he said, be even unintentionally rude to one. And for one whose life was literature, who in the end found everything else turn to vapour as negotiable as the Watts sisters floating up and down the stairs at The Pines in their cloudy bonnets and mantles, he was a rigid stickler for all the little formalities of nice existence. Years later, he was to rebuke his dear old friend William Rossetti gently but stiffly for having written, in an account of his first meeting with the Pre-Raphaelite painters at the Oxford Union, that he had 'introduced himself' to Gabriel. 'I never (allow me to say) introduced myself to anybody, and certainly should not have done so in my nonage'. Perish the thought! It was one thing to circulate ribald witticisms among close, trusting friends, but the idea of mixed gatherings of people to whom he had never been introduced going into fits of laughter over Howell's doubtful anecdotes was repulsive to him. He hastened to put Gosse right on the story, which Gosse must have already heard going the rounds in London. 'That polecat, Howell,' he called his former friend with unabated loathing years afterwards. Of all the vermin whose predatory squeakings were now breaking into the long green afternoon peace of The Pines—Gabriel had prophesied shrewdly, only he had thought that Swinburne's reputation might be damaged later, after they were all dead—Howell would remain 'the vilest wretch that I, at all events, ever came across'.

In the same letter to Gosse, Swinburne spoke scornfully of another and far more pathetic discarded friend of his bohemian youth—the gifted Jewish artist, Simeon Solomon, a homosexual whose wonderfully bright morning had ended abruptly. Not possessing the amusing blackguard Howell's talents for just keeping on the right side of the law, Solomon had run into trouble and a gaol sentence in 1873. His dog-like devotion to Swinburne had made him only too eager to

turn out the drawings of flogging blocks and victims suggested by the author of 'Atalanta', who was in his turn
passing on the compulsive promptings of the author of such
shot rubbish as 'The School-boy's Tragedy'. After the
scandal, Swinburne had hastily dropped him; his references
to homosexuality, made to Watts and other friends, are
always uncompromisingly hostile. They may have been part
of his constant preoccupation with proving to himself his
own virility, by accepting the challenge of the unclimbed
cliff, the stormiest sea, the most testing physical pain. But it
is hard not to see Solomon as a sort of sacrifice, and hard not
to hear in Swinburne's remarks about him the first note
which reminds one regretfully of Prince Hal. Poor Solomon,
the friend of Walter Pater and Oscar Browning, died in 1905
in a London workhouse, an alcoholic, deserted by all, pursued by the relentless Furies.

Now, Swinburne wrote Gosse from The Pines, Solomon
was said to be hawking round for sale his letters which were
full of 'silly chaff indulged in long ago'. What happened to
them is still a mystery. The scholars and the universities
have gathered into their laps every least flower and weed
from Swinburne's grave, as Rossetti foretold they would,
but the brilliant garlands that were flung from time to time
over Solomon's gratified head have vanished. Perhaps the
world contains a secret hoarder of Swinburniana, first
cousin to the crazy millionaire collector with an under-
ground gallery of stolen masters over which he gloats in the
small hours. Perhaps the indefatigable Watts sought out
Solomon and bought the letters back. After Rossetti died, he
discreetly negotiated for the return of some of Swinburne's
letters to Gabriel, which were in the rapacious trunk of the
Elephant, Fanny Schott, who also threatened to sell them.
In 1885, an antiquarian bookseller and publisher, George
Redway, wrote to Swinburne to say that eighteen of the

poet's now famous letters to Charles Augustus Howell were
in his possession, adding in casual fashion that he would be
glad of a new poem from Mr. Swinburne for an anthology
of river-and-sea-songs that he was planning. The invaluable
friend padded out again from Putney and some months
later, after dickering at which we can only guess, retrieved
the letters, in exchange for which he had agreed with Mr.
Redway to swap the copyright of the patriotic poem 'A
Word for the Navy'. (Chatto bought it from Redway in
1896.) One can imagine the scene when he brought the
bundle, dog-eared now with appreciative reading, back to
The Pines. The friends shut themselves up in the back
library, and Swinburne's hands shook and jiggled more than
ever as he turned over the pages of scrawling writing. (How
his handwriting changed during the years of his life with
Watts, by the way! In his youth it may or may not have
resembled de Sade's, but it sprawled wildly every way at
once, with long tails and loops and blotted crossing-outs. In
his letters from The Pines, the calligraphy is that of a careful
school-boy, clear and neat.) Then at night, after the household was asleep in bed, after Algernon himself was safely
retired and reading by the light of the candles in his three
brass candle-sticks—with which he somehow miraculously
contrived to escape absent-mindedly setting the bed, himself
and the room on fire—Watts went softly downstairs to the
nether regions presided over by Dido, the dog, who thumped
her tail in surprised welcome at the unusual sight. Hetty, or
the current Hetty and her friend, could be heard snoring
gently in their nest off the passage where the house bells
hung along the wall like a bar of crotchets. Here were all the
comfortable domestic smells of The Pines, the lingering
whiffs of roast meat and apples aromatic with cloves beneath
browning pie-crust that I had seemed to catch the other
day, wafting up to the odd little tower-room and staying

there like an imprisoned household spirit, a fruity concentrated bouquet of the past stoppered down under the roof. The black beetles popped back beneath the dresser as Watts approached the still warm kitchen range—it was July, and no fires for consuming past indiscretions would be lit in the grates upstairs. Quietly and methodically, probably attired in a frock-coat, Watts raised the cover, thrust the package of letters into the embers, and thankfully set light to them.

Or did he? For that is one of the greatest mysteries over which The Pines presides, the respectable little widow sitting thinking of her two late husbands behind her blue medallion of illustrious widowhood, while the world passes indifferently by her gate. 'Not at home', had been the message I seemed to hear murmured when I had been given a glimpse behind her demure veil. And 'Not on your life' was the crisper answer I got when, paying another call on the Relict of Putney Hill, I somehow trusted to her resident phantasmagoria to provide a few hints, to be kind enough to a, by now, so thoroughly implicated observer as to play out in the empty air a dumb show of the comedy or tragedy or near infamy that took place here on a July day eighty-three years ago. 'An elderly lady in deep mourning,' the gentler but still rebuking whisper resumed, 'is surely entitled to keep some drawers locked. And since all the scholars, the writers who have visited me over the years with somewhat impertinent questions about Mr. Swinburne and Mr. Watts-Dunton have been forced to go away admitting that I, and only I, hold the key to this particular fascinating little secret compartment, I suggest that you withdraw without troubling me or yourself further, and close my door as quietly as possible behind you when you leave.'

The answer which The Pines returns to too curious pilgrims on this particular score is certainly justified, for nobody else knows what exactly happened to the notorious

Howell letters. Watts was said to have brought them back to his friend—the trusty dog bounding along with the retrieved quarry in his soft, experienced mouth makes a charming Landseer-like composition—and it was assumed that he destroyed them. Yet after Swinburne's death, the damaging letters written by a great poet in his wild youth to a polecat proved to have been carefully laid up, in lavender or civet, at The Pines. Then Watts had only pretended to burn them? The stealthy nocturnal descent to the kitchen vanishes into thin air. Ha ha! cried the enemies of the pearl most perfect found in all the sea. Watts' single-minded determination to set Swinburne's genius out of reach of the polecats seems to have been flawed after all. Was the flaw cupidity? The letters naturally had their price for eager collectors of Swinburnian 'curiosities', and Watts sold them. But were they or were they not the identical ones written to Howell for which Watts bargained away 'A Word for the Navy'? Or had Watts burnt what he considered the worst, in his cautious lawyer's view, and retained only the eighteen surviving specimens, with Swinburne's knowledge and at his express wish, so that he could keep them locked in his desk and read them occasionally, 'to change the cold heart of the weary time' that had to be filled somehow in the silence of The Pines? It is possible. For one gets the impression that the dull solicitor of so many legends, the 'old horror of Putney', as Edmund Gosse later referred to him, who was supposed to hold Swinburne mesmerized in semi-sinister captivity at The Pines, understood the needs of human flesh and blood well enough, even when they wandered off in peculiar directions. The nut-brown eyes of the frock-coated lay-figure, bright as those of some creature peering out of a bank of fern and foxglove, saw a number of things very plainly, we may be sure. There was a strong vein of mysticism in him. Passion, mystery, ecstasy were not beyond his comprehension. If it were not so, a man of Swinburne's warm, impulsive temperament could not have endured thirty years of living under the same roof, or corresponded with him, when they were apart, with such affectionate ease, as though plunging his arms into a favourite old coat which knew him in every wrinkle and gave more comfort, more latitude to sudden changes of temperature or movement, than any other garment in his wardrobe.

Yet when his beloved and childishly trusting friend died, Watts produced the letters to Howell and sold them? Yes, he did. The Pines pulls a scarf of mist round her shoulders, averts her gaze, puts out her lights, and sticks a card in the bow window beneath the curled and horned satyr's mask: 'No callers; gone to bed'. Everything is too mixed at this distance to be sure of anything. When the bundle of old gossip and jokes and indecencies left her roof, they were eventually consigned to Sir Edmund Gosse's obliging friend, Posterity, who receives all secrets with large liberality and discretion in the capacious pigeonhole reserved for her in the majestic halls of the British Museum. Before that final re-direction, Sir Edmund read them with renewed sighs for the frequent incomprehensible ability of men of genius, so many of whom had been his friends, to have profiles that do not match—on the right side of their faces, a noble sweetness, a lofty idealism, and yet, turn the coin, and there is the bewildering imprint of the curled and horned goaty god. And such a ridiculous breed of goatiness too! That was why poor Gosse avoided even a hint in his excellent but somehow incomplete portrait of Swinburne and had to post pained postscripts to Posterity admitting that he had shrunk from depicting the warts. He had no such hesitation in castigating the friend who he claimed had failed to destroy these letters. He hoped that they would now be firmly, irrevocably, faithfully destroyed. They were not. The purchaser was none other than his valued and unquestioned fellow-worker in the fields of Swinburniana, the extraordinary forger, Thomas J. Wise. Whatever he may have told Gosse, the letters stayed intact in Wise's collection. After his death, when they made their final journey to the British Museum, they were kept packaged away, signed, sealed, and carefully guarded from casual prurient eyes. The Swinburne scholars who had been permitted to view them deemed them 'unpublishable', until everything became mixed again, and they were given in their unexpurgated entirety in the six volumes of the Yale University Press edition of the 'Letters', edited by Cecil Y. Lang, which were published between 1959 and 1962.

## V

'WILL FRIDAY—to-day week—suit you to receive us?' wrote Swinburne in July, 1884, to Mrs. Anne Ritchie, Thackeray's gay and delightful daughter, who was living not far off in Wimbledon. 'It is the day which would best suit Mr. Watts; to me, who never go anywhere, all days are usually alike.' Watts is the man of affairs who meets new people and goes out and about (though not so much, to be sure, as the gregarious diner-out would have liked), but Swinburne has begun the process of deliberate detachment that by the turn of the century will have become absolute. To Mrs. Ritchie—a dear friend since her girlhood days when she and her sister, rapturously giggling, had listened to young Mr. Swinburne shrilling 'Les Noyades' to a dumbfounded after-dinner gathering, which included the Archbishop of York, at Lord Houghton's Yorkshire home—he was simply offering a piece of information, without complaining or wishing that it were different. His refusal to repine was one of his greatest virtues.

> I would not bid thee, though I might, give back
> One good thing youth has given and borne away;
> I crave not any comfort of the day
> That is not, nor on time's retrodden track
> Would turn to meet the white-robed hours or black
> That long since left me on their mortal way. . .

'A Vision of Spring in Winter' had been written when he was a wintry thirty-eight. Now he was forty-seven, and he appeared to be stoically going forward, practically at running pace, to meet old age. He and Watts, two middle-aged bachelors, had left the uncertain spring behind and were thankfully settled side by side in front of the fire at The Pines. Watts, we are told, by his biographers, Thomas Hake and Arthur Compton-Rickett, hardly changed in appearance after that. 'He had grown old at forty', and the broad, calm forehead remained unwrinkled to the end; the whole face stayed round and rosy as a good keeping apple, slightly withered but still wholesome on its shelf. He and Swinburne had now lived together for five years, and their joint household resembled, in all particulars but sex, a steady and successful homosexual union. Swinburne was the docile stay-at-home 'wife', Watts was the 'husband' who managed all their business affairs, dictated the decisions, and doled out the pin-money. No woman, it was clear, would ever enter the picture now. Swinburne had apparently not thought of marriage again since the disastrous death of the heart which he had suffered when he was twenty-five. Though he supplied a cardiogram to what had happened to him in the passionate, self-castigating lament 'The Triumph of Time', his biographers disagree in their readings. According to Edmund Gosse, he had been rejected, with wounding peals of nervous laughter at the little suitor's twitching limbs and shrill voice, by a young lady called Jane Faulkner, nicknamed 'Boo'. But later researchers have rejected 'Boo' herself, since a Swinburne scholar, Mr. John S. Mayfield of Syracuse University, tracked her down and revealed that she was hardly out of the nursery when Swinburne was supposed to have fallen in love with her. They insist that the girl was his beloved cousin, Mary Gordon, who scribbled verse and rode and acted in uproarious family theatricals with him in the blissful early days at East Dene. She had married an older man, Colonel Disney Leith of the 106th

68

Light Infantry, in 1865. The mature military figure, the triumphant flesh-and-blood reality of Algernon's old ineffectual boyish dreams of joining the Dragoons, bears her off into a happy fishing-and-shooting life in Scotland. Silence closes down, maternity closes down, and she does not reappear until, wearing a widow's cap, she visits her old cousin at The Pines in the nineties. This lady fiercely denied any sentimental attachment between them other than deep ties of family affection, which may have been the cause of her wish—piously fulfilled, and calling down on her head the rage of all collectors of Swinburniana—that her priceless collection of the intimate letters he wrote to her, his mother, and two of his sisters, should be burnt after she, the only survivor, died (she had edited a small volume of tantalizingly brief extracts). The bonfire was duly made some time after her death in 1926. All that appears with certainty in the light of its flames is that Swinburne's visits to the Amazons in St. John's Wood and the start of the wild, compulsive drinking date from the mid-sixties.

What could not be burnt by any loyal self-appointed censor are his two novels, 'Lesbia Brandon' (though Watts successfully vetoed its publication in their lifetime, and the cautious Gosse seems to have agreed) and 'Love's Cross-Currents', and the blank-verse autobiographical play, 'The Sisters', which he wrote looking back at the past from Putney when he was fifty-five. Herbert in the first work, and the two Reginalds, 'Redgie' Harewood and Reggie Clavering, who are the heroes of the other novel and the verse-drama, are clearly Algernon Swinburne. In all of them we are in a world which has an odd, haunting familiarity until we realize it is the world of an Ivy Compton-Burnett novel, in which well-bred voices murmur under the elms, where the family are taking tea. The butler carries away the silver tray, croquet balls click on the summer air, and the civilized voices murmur some more, but suddenly the lawn seems to open, fire and brimstone spout, and the butler reappears with the visiting card of one of the Eumenides, who is now waiting, smoothing her skirts, in the drawing-room. Against the country-house background of his youth— a vivid blend of his own home, the Gordons' nearby house, Northcourt, in the Isle of Wight, and autumn visits to his extraordinary old grandfather, Sir John Swinburne, at Capheaton Hall in Northumberland—Swinburne set his obsessive personal themes of disturbing relationships going on all the time under the smooth upper-class Victorian surface, of implacable old dowagers arranging the lives of other people as calmly as though they are pieces on a solitaire board, of the child of an adulterous affair conveniently becoming heir to his supposed father's title before any scandal breaks, of masochistic passions always, and of erotic situations between two young people, tied closely in kinship (in 'Lesbia Brandon' they are brother and sister, in 'The Sisters' they are cousins), who cannot follow their emotions through into marriage.

Whatever the love disappointment had been, it produced a trauma about marriage which lasted all Swinburne's life. 'When I hear that a personal friend has fallen into matrimonial courses, I feel the same sorrow as if I had heard of him lapsing into theism', he had written to a correspondent in 1878. More wistfully, he had sent his congratulations to Edmund Gosse when Gosse married Miss Nellie Epps three years earlier. 'I suppose it must be the best thing that can befall a man to win and keep the woman that he loves while they are yet young.' That particular happiness, he said, he was 'now never likely to share'.

Watts may have suffered a similar early disappointment over a girl, but his biographers have kept it dark. According to them, Literature and Nature were the beautiful twin sisters whom he worshipped equally from his very different youth up, as Pope managed to divide his ardour simultaneously between the ravishing Blount girls, Martha and Teresa. Yet we may suspect that the 'eminently respectable suburban solicitor, conservative of taste and habits', 'in heart in the suburbs with Mrs. Grundy, worshipping propriety as personified by Tennyson', of whom many of those visiting The Pines made a little obvious fun, though not quite knowing what to do with the inconvenient wild stray in that capacious brain, like a single flaunting poppy seeded in a conventional garden, of his curious romantic fixation on the gypsies, their lore and their language—we may suspect that this solid, self-contained man was not impervious to women. He liked them pretty. When he visited Italy in the seventies, he wrote to Swinburne in London that Venice had particularly captivated him, not only for its beauty, but because he noticed three pretty faces on his walks for every one encountered in other Italian cities. Beneath that waterfall of a brown moustache, drowned in the cascade of 'clotted' hair, as one caller at The Pines, A. C. Benson, has described it, there was a sensuous mouth which can be better observed in earlier pictures, before shagginess descended. His poems about men and women, supplied with careful Romany glossaries, abound in ripe lips and trim, tempting shapes of *rinkeni* (handsome) gypsy *chis* (girls), to whom his hero whispers '*Minaw!* (My own!)'.

> Pouring through all my frame a life divine
> From Rhona's throbbing bosom claspt to mine. . .
> And when upon my neck she fell, my love,
> Her hair smelt sweet of whin and woodland spice. . .

Perhaps something had happened to him as it had happened to Swinburne. It may be that one of these whin-scented Rhonas or Sinfis, about whom he loved to ramble on to sympathetic callers until Swinburne's eyes glazed over with boredom, had dealt him a mortal blow from which he never fully recovered, or after which he took to the single-minded rescue of heroes. The moustache grew, the mouth hid itself prudently in the thicket. But Watts is always capable of surprises. If we reject such theories and decide to believe in the dull and jealous duenna of a brilliant charge, the extinguisher of a burning flame, as hinted by Gosse in the 'Life' with outward deference but occasional tiny sharp stabs of the pen, Watts steps out of character just as we thought we had got him settled. Watts, we are told by Robert Speaight in his life of the painter, William Rothenstein, once took a cab in which, at a discreet distance, to follow the promenade of a 'stunner' whom he admired. The stunner was the radiant young actress, Alice Kingsley, the daughter of the Pre-Raphaelite painter and pupil of Rossetti, Walter Knewstub, who later married Rothenstein. Watts knelt on the floor of the cab so that, if the glorious creature happened to look back, she would not easily recognize its occupant prospecting her, or merely see his head served up like St. John the Baptist on a platter. It is a ridiculous position, and we would admire him more if he had followed the young woman boldly on foot, but the episode seems to show that Mr. Watts had a susceptible heart. He appeared to have suppressed it long ago in order to give himself up, with a stoicism perhaps as great as Swinburne's own, to the difficult business of being guardian and servant to genius in Putney.

Watts had rescued the divine bow of Apollo and its owner, but the hardest part of his task came later, as often happens, when the extreme crisis was over and all that remained was to keep both safely employed at The Pines. Now, and for the rest of their lives together, he must try to indicate directions (preferably profitable ones) in which to aim the shafts. So many vistas were closed, their great trees felled, their statues overthrown in the grass. Mazzini was dead, and the gods and the nymphs had flown. Yet Swinburne's health was better than it had ever been, and his vigour, carefully guarded by an inflexible time-table, was prodigious. The arrows flew out of the study window at The Pines in an astonishing shower and in all directions—poetry, drama, literary essays for the reviews and the Encyclopædia Britannica, political tirades, thundering letters to the press denouncing his enemies and the enemies of Literature. Watts had his work cut out to gather them up and bear them off to market. If some of them did not absolutely reach the mark—how could they? for heaven's gift of infallibility hardly ever lasts a mortal span, and perhaps those critics are right who hold that Swinburne's genius suffered a subtle and serious injury, from which it never fully recovered, in the groves of the rapacious chastising goddesses in the sixties —Watts was always on hand to praise the marksmanship and to assure him that aim and style had never been more masterly. 'Watts says it is *the* best poem I ever wrote', Swinburne would report cheerfully to his mother and sisters. 'Watts praises both the design and (thus far) the performance to the skies—in terms which I will not quote lest you should be reminded of the glowing praises recorded by Mrs. Gamp as having so "frequent" been bestowed on her by Mrs. Harris'. 'I shall be glad if you like the play as well or half as well as Watts does. He *is* satisfactory.'

He was indeed. Watts says, Watts thinks and I agree—the phrases are threaded through his letters as liberally as the Gamp-ese, the lines from Shakespeare and the Bible, the classical allusions, and the obscure Elizabethan jests. In time the satisfactory friend's praise flowed almost automatically (as on one embarrassing occasion, when he rashly referred in print to 'Mr. Swinburne's noble sonnet' on a dead friend, which he had not had time to read, and which turned out, alas, to be not one of Algernon's best works). By then, Swinburne bathed in the renewing fountain so happily that he could hardly put pen to paper without dipping into it at every stage of a poem. Later, it seems that he even needed, Walter's approval of what he was going to say in the presumed confidence of a letter to a friend. 'Walter has read and cordially agrees with every word of the above', he writes contentedly to Edmund Gosse, for instance, and we can imagine without difficulty what kind of expression snapped and glinted behind Gosse's spectacles as *he* read.

And was Watts really to blame, as his enemies said he was, for supplying such an abundance of the stimulating appreciation which Swinburne needed, and not applying the brake to his fatal fluency, or, as Lady Jane sadly and wisely put it in one of the occasional confidential letters she wrote to her son's friend, his fault of 'not knowing where to stop'? There was much that he wrote at The Pines that merited all Watts' admiration. Sometimes the arrow sped through the air with the old, superb rush of musical sound and, for us, a sense of the hand launching and the brain beautifully controlling it. But there was more, much more, for which the best words seem to be those a perceptive Dutch novelist, Maarten Maartens, used after he had paid a visit to the little couple at The Pines in the nineties. Swinburne took a fancy to him and expressed it by reeling off, as a mark of favour, the whole of the extremely long poem on the doom of the two knightly Northumbrian brothers, Balen and Balan, who served King Arthur and slew one another unwittingly in combat. The metre of 'The Tale of Balen', melodious for a lyrical subject, ends by falling on a listener's ear with the exhausting monotony of torture by water. Swinburne was incapable of believing that others might not share his own rapturous delight in declaiming his own song. When, in his youth, he had first met his idolized Mazzini, he had seized Mazzini's hand, kissed it, and then carolled into the leader's ear the more than seven hundred lines of the 'Song of Italy'. Poor old Landor had reeled under the weight of the little young poet's homage in 1864. Now, as Maarten Maartens sat in the book-lined room gravely listening, Swinburne was a little elderly poet, but nothing else had changed. He still never knew where to stop. And for his chanting delivery of 'Balen', the sympathetic Dutchman found a description which seems to apply to so much of Swinburne's poetry in the thirty years of life with Watts, '. . . too subjective an outpour, and wearisomely impassioned, like a child's jump against a wall.'

Yet, he did not quite know how it was, the moment the ordeal was over and the clear, high-pitched voice stopped warbling, the visitor felt 'a poignant grief' that it had ceased. He got up, said good-bye to the Dickensian little pair in their carpet slippers, glanced in farewell round the 'dull temple of a rainbow muse', and walked out into Putney. It had been strangely lovely while it lasted, like a tormenting but unforgettable affair, and he used an erotic metaphor to describe the experience of Swinburne singing in the flesh instead of in print: 'All the difference between seeing a beautiful woman and feeling her embraces.'

*     *     *

When we look back at Swinburne's methodical day-to-day routine at The Pines, it strikes us as having the monotony and isolation of life on board ship, which many people, after all, find extremely agreeable. Sleeping, eating, walking, eating again, sleeping again, working in one's cabin, mixing with the other passengers for a while in the lounge, perhaps another little turn round the deck before dinner, more reading, lights out. Then next day it starts off once more, only varied by the changes of the waves and winds, an extra-ordinary dream one had in one's deck chair just before the cups of consommé came round, or the excitement of an occasional ship on the horizon. Sleeping, eating, walking, thinking—so the voyage went on for thirty years. It may be that some academic Swinburnian computer has made it its business to calculate the number of miles he must have covered in that time on or around Putney Heath—or 'moor', as he preferred to call it, perhaps thinking of Emily Brontë, a sister spirit—as serious shipboard promenaders tot up their score of circuits of the boat-deck.

Swinburne, racing along every morning from eleven o'clock to lunchtime, passing like a somnambulist through the traffic and rain, shine, or the London subfusc that is neither, noted the changing seasons carefully, for Watts had suggested Nature as a rich subject for new lyrics. The familiar daily round was soothing and never boring. His comments upon it become increasingly parochial. When Churton Collins went along with him one day, they walked to a favourite spot from which they looked down into the vale, its great trees anchored in deep pasturage, quietly sleeping away its last period of rural reprieve before London pushed noisily nearer, the twentieth century arrived, the hay-makers in Wimbledon Park would pack up for the last time, and presently along would come the little red lines of houses, the roads scything through the green, and the cars devouring them. Swinburne thought it 'as fine as anything in England', he said to Collins. And when his old friend Mrs. Eliza Lynn Linton, the novelist, whose rather formidable spectacled face would always be an object of veneration and affection to him because she had been the 'spiritual daugh-ter' of his spiritual master, Walter Savage Landor, in Landor's last years—when Mrs. Linton wrote cracking up the scenery in Palermo, back went the firm answer: 'I doubt if you have seen anything there to match our Putney sunsets.'

But the great natural event of the local year, which never failed to delight him, was the moment in May when the wild hawthorn thickets spread out their delicious rustic feast (as they still do to-day on the Putney and Wimbledon commons) of thick clotted white, piled high in shining green cornucopias, with here and there an even more delectable pyramid, their curds seemingly tinged with a swirl of raspberry juice. Roses are the flowers that twine themselves all through the poems of Swinburne's youth. At Putney the hawthorns haunted him, as they queened it over the 'Méséglise way' for Proust at Combray. He hymned the gladness of waiting for their appearance, the joy of visiting them every day at their radiant fresh perfection, and his melancholy when they were over for another year. In spite of his long love affair with them, Swinburne's hawthorn hedges do not smell so divinely or stand shedding their light and perfume mysteriously forever as Proust's do. He is never as good at writing about flowers as he is describing the emotions of a return to the arms of the sea.

In the summer The Pines seemed stuffy and airless. The hot weather was always a penance to him as he grew older. He wilted and longed for the annual holiday that he and Watts took for several years running in lodgings at various seaside places. The fixed hours of hotel meals and the curious stares of other holiday folk were not for them. They preferred to find rooms in 'a decent cottage' where they could come and go as they liked. Their decorous bathing costumes packed among the books and the weekly reviews (but Swinburne liked, whenever possible, to go out in a boat and swim naked), they journeyed over the years to Sark and Guernsey, to Shoreham and Eastbourne on the south coast and Cromer on the east coast. Swinburne's rapture over these reunions

77

with his 'nursing mother' was as passionate as the delight
of the daughter of earth, rising from the dark regions of
Pluto and finding once more the crocus by the brook and the
nightingales singing among the olives. His family home was
never again to be by the sea. We do not know why Captain
(as he was then) Swinburne suddenly decided to leave East
Dene in 1864 and move his family to the mainland. Was it
that the kindly, unimaginative sailor's eye had yet taken
anxious note of Algernon riding over so continually to the
Gordons at Northcourt? The ties of kinship, he may have
felt, were too dangerously interwoven to encourage anything closer. He and Lady Jane were second cousins;
Algernon and his high-spirited, gifted cousin were closely
related on both the paternal and maternal side. We cannot
tell, and to the question, East Dene, like The Pines on
another occasion when discourteously pressed for an answer,
looks steadfastly in another direction on her high lawns
above the sea among her dark ilex trees and elms noisy with
rook colonies. Whatever prompted Captain Swinburne to
make the move, the house was sold to a wealthy Manchester
textile man, John Snowden Henry, who was said to have
spent ninety thousand pounds on vulgarizing and darkening
what we may guess were light rooms of charming Regency
simplicity, building a massive lodge and other additions,
and scattering his coat of arms and twined initials liberally
over walls and ceilings. 'A damned ghost revisiting earth.'
So Swinburne had felt, he wrote desolately, when he had
returned to the Isle of Wight in 1873 for the first time since
the sale to stay with his Gordon aunt and uncle. To him it
would always be the earthly paradise. There would never be
another place which he loved as deeply as he had loved East
Dene. Perhaps there would be no sea, even the grandeur of
the coast of Sark and Guernsey that he praised so ecstatic-
ally, to eclipse the memory of those ravishing, ever-chang-

ing seascapes of blue and purple, of steel and sullen foam specks, storm and salt fog, that Bonchurch had spread at his feet when he was a boy, galloping up and down the steep slopes on his pony.

But the seaside holidays still recaptured the old joy, and it overflowed in poetry, some of the loveliest and most intensely felt of his land-locked Putney years.

> A purer passion, a lordlier leisure,
> A peace more happy than lives on land,
> Fulfils with pulse of diviner pleasure
> The dreaming head and the steering hand.
> I lean my cheek to the cold grey pillow,
> The deep soft swell of the full broad billow,
> And close mine eyes for delight past measure,
> And wish the wheel of the world would stand.

The wheel bears him, reddened by salt and sun, and Watts, more like a gypsy than ever, back to The Pines, and soon, walking on his moor, he notes that the lake is frozen hard and covered with charming flocks of skaters. London appears to be imitating Siberia, he writes to his fascinating Russian-born nihilist friend and translator of his poems, Madame Tola Dorian, in Paris, where he had met her in 1882 when he and Watts took their one and only jaunt abroad for the fiftieth anniversary of the first performance of Victor Hugo's *Le Roi s'Amuse*. Little Bertie Mason, the child at The Pines, has an atrocious cold and is not allowed to go out and enjoy himself in the snowdrifts with other Putney urchins. And almost the next minute, so it seems to the walker on Putney Heath, it is Spring again and the hawthorns are begininng to put out their little leaves in preparation for the great breathtaking May festival.

When it came to suggesting new sources of inspiration for his friend to follow, it was inevitable that Watts, the dedicated Child of the Open Air, should commend Swinburne earnestly to Nature, the splendid untamed power after whom he used to tramp through Richmond Park with George Borrow and his enormous green umbrella, listening respectfully to the great man's musings on the ways of birds, roe-deer, and Romany women, and calling in at the Bald-faced Stag inn in Kingston Vale to refresh themselves with pints of 'swipes', as Borrow called light ale. Had not Mr. Watts senior been known round St. Ives as the Gilbert White of the Ouse Valley? The bookish solicitor who had enjoyed pottering his spare afternoons away observing the creeping and flying life going on unconcernedly in the reedy margins of the Ouse, and who died suddenly and happily, a healthy old man, coming home from such a walk in 1884, had passed on those tastes to his son. Watts wrote deplorable nature poetry himself. Swinburne stayed in his room, breakfasting and reading, until ten o'clock, but Watts was up between five and six all through the year, lit his own fire in winter, made his tea and boiled the egg left out for him by the current Hetty, and then was off to Wimbledon Common to startle the birds and the townships of scudding rabbits. He was an admirer of Thoreau, though Borrow had referred rather nastily to 'the Yankee Hermit'. Once he made a rendezvous with Christina Rossetti to escort her to watch the sun rising, after the poetess had admitted that she had never seen the phenomenon before. The grey sky became apple-green and lilac; up came the sun and changed all the cows lying chewing in the thick chilly mist to beasts of burnished copper reclining on a field of the cloth of gold. Yes, Miss Rossetti gravely allowed, 'a sunrise surpassed a sunset and was worth getting up to see'. Watts felt with scientific satisfaction that dear Christina's description of a dawn would be more authentic in future, though he was pretty certain (with one of those quick flashes of understanding of other people's ways) that she would never trouble to get up to see another as long as she lived.

But he urged Swinburne to be authentic, too, to hoard accurate observations thriftily on his walks and on their joint midsummer excursions to the sea. He must become the laureate of Watts' patron deity, wonderful Natura Benigna. Swinburne seems to have needed no urging. He fell in with the suggestion so enthusiastically that we find him exclaiming in a letter to his sister Alice that 'if only poor Coleridge could—if only poor Rossetti could—have taken the same wholesome and happy and grateful delight in Nature as Wordsworth and Tennyson did, and as Walter and I do, they would have been so much happier—and (I hope and think) such much better men'. The sentiments doubtless gratified Miss Alice, of whom we have a delightful photograph taken in middle-age—a plump, unmistakably Swinburne lady dressed in a braided tailored suit, sitting pensively with a bit of Nature in the shape of a pet parrot perched on her knee. Though addressed to this approving family audience, they have a touch of that odd Prince Hal priggishness, very alien to Swinburne, which something in the stuffy air of The Pines seems to bring out. Poor Coleridge had been enslaved by opium, poor Rossetti by chloral, but Swinburne, having thrown off his infirmity, is sitting in Putney as a member of an exclusive club along with Wordsworth and Tennyson and Walter, endlessly celebrating the wholesome nourishing mother of them all. He is happy—there is no doubt about that. For the rest of his life he continued to sing—sometimes splendidly, sometimes so mechanically and verbosely that Nature stiffens up and puts on an 'expression', says nothing, smells of nothing, does not move a flat painted leaf or flower—of the sea and the hawthorns, the strong orange-eyed seamews dipping down over the edge of cliffs alight with 'poppies red as love or shame', and particularly of lonely, encircled places, bays or lakes surrounded by a matrix of crags lying in 'the strong compulsive silence of the sun', where a swimmer could rejoice in the coming peace of the dark waters waiting to enfold him below. It became a stoical major theme of the Putney years.

## VI

ANOTHER SOURCE of inspiration turned out to be close at hand for study in the unpromising Pre-Raphaelite clutter of The Pines. It was the logical outcome—the isolation of Putney must have concentrated it and loosened a screw or two—of Swinburne's lifelong fondness for the very old and the very young. Though he 'never went anywhere' and disliked parties, he wrote to one of his women friends, the wife of William Rossetti, 'more than ever as I get older and deafer', there were still welcoming houses of married friends—kind, dependable William and his Lucy, the Gosses, Ned and Georgiana Burne-Jones in Fulham—to which he enjoyed paying a quiet visit with Watts, being made much of, and, above all, admiring the latest additions to their young families. If ever there was a loving father *manqué* it was Swinburne. It is a pity that the Swinburne procreative strain—so lusty in that ancestress who was one of the famous landmarks of Northumberland through having given birth to thirty live, thriving children by one husband, and still, in the previous generation, sturdy enough to assemble twenty-four grandchildren at one noisy go for autumn reunions at Capheaton Hall—seemed to be thinning out. It is a great pity that our photograph of Swinburne's sister Alice does not show her proudly perching a first grandchild on her breadth of serge skirt instead of a parrot. It is really a thousand pities that she and Charlotte and Isabel never married and presented him with housefuls of nephews and nieces to whom he would have been the overwhelmingly favourite uncle, the wonderful giver of presents, the teller of endless tales fetched up from oblivion and stored, in mint condition and ready to hand, in that marvellous warehouse of a memory. It was sad that they were, as he ruefully said he was, 'a barren stock'.

Cheerful, industrious maiden-ladies, they did not seem in the least rueful about their condition. The strong ties of family affection that bound them all, and Swinburne too, maybe sufficed. They stayed in Wiltshire and helped their mother to entertain the relatives who dropped in for those exhausting Victorian visitations of a month or so; nursed Lady Jane devotedly when she was ill; taught the lodge-keeper's children their pothooks and sums; played the piano; exchanged long loving letters with The Pines; and laughed a great deal over Algernon's readings of 'Tristram Shandy' as they sat with their needlework in the summer evenings of one of his visits. Very occasionally they went to London for an art exhibition, or the Handel Festival. Such were the short and simple annals of the gentle unmarried woman in the Misses Swinburne's day, and they seemed to accept their limitations with something of their brother's stoicism. Abba daringly once left supervising the pothooks long enough to scribble a short story, encouraged by kind Mr. Watts. Lady Jane mentioned it rather crushingly in one of her letters to Algernon's invaluable friend who was being so helpful with her over business affairs. He was about to become co-trustee, with the family solicitor, Mr. Long-bourne, of her will, such things being, as she said, 'quite out of his (Algernon's) line'. 'I was sure you would be disappointed with Isabel's little story,' Lady Jane went on, 'for I knew that she was not able to do anything worth publishing.' It may be an echo of the old idea that a woman writing or trying to write was somewhat ridiculous. And perhaps Watts was disappointed, for we hear no more of Abba's effort. The fire-bird only swooped down once on this tranquil English roof-tree. There was to be no other dazzling foreign flash of plumage across the croquet lawn.

Swinburne's passion for the whole 'race of babies' was not in the least like the calm kindliness with which we can picture Ally and Abba bending over the slates of the good little creatures from the lodge. It may have started, as the Swinburnian scholars have told us, in his admiration for Blake's songs of childhood and Victor Hugo's *L'Art d'être grandpère*. But there was nothing of the grandfather, or at least of the British grandfather, in the idolatry of the infant world which was heightened and became a little too generous with incense, more than a little dotty, in the first decade of his years at The Pines. Calm and kindly it was not. There was something oddly voracious about it, as his drinking habits had been said to be in his youth—a sort of thirsty delight in the solemn pink faces surrounded by plush bonnets, the waving fingers and toes, the occasional toothless beams which he sampled, peeping into the perambulators of the nursemaids on Putney Heath. They were as intoxicating as the hawthorns, and not nearly as faithless. As one bundle left its baby-chariot, staggered uncertainly across the grass and then ran and finally disappeared towards the prison shades of the class-room, another delightful object was sure to take its place. Victorian nurseries were unfailing cornucopias of babyhood. His letters to the sympathetic Wiltshire audience of women frequently describe some adorable 'Chick' encountered on a walk. Lady Jane believed in her pious heart that Algernon's love of children might 'lead to the faith of his youth in some hidden way'. She was wrong, but the hope made her encourage him in return to indulge still more extravagantly.

The children of his friends were always reliably getting themselves born and requiring a graceful letter of welcome to them and congratulation to their fortunate parents. Swinburne longed, he would write, to kiss the feet of the new arrival. In their innocent fashion, these crumpled, rosy godlings and godling-esses seem to be carrying on the delicious tyranny of the fair Amazons in St. John's Wood. He abased himself happily before them. At the same time, he refused firmly all requests to stand godfather. Much later in life, he explained his still deeply felt antagonism to the symbolism of Christian baptism in making his excuses to a distant cousin, Lady Henniker Heaton, who had asked him to sponsor a new daughter at the font. Though 'greatly honoured', he repeated how impossible it would be for him 'to take any part, direct or indirect, in a religious ceremony which represents [a new-born baby] as "a child of wrath"— words which seem to me the most horrible of all blasphemies —standing in need of human intervention to transmute it into "a child of grace" '. But he would often drop into the cradle of an old friend's infant a lovely little song or a shapely roundel in place of a coral rattle or a silver teething-ring. When the babes occasionally died in infancy, he fashioned smooth monuments of verse for them. The charms of the strikingly good-looking Rossetti family; Sylvia Gosse; a beautiful little dark-eyed niece of Watts, Olive, who at nine years old was already a 'stunner'—he celebrated them all. And he had a sure, instinctive touch with children. They showed a gratifying partiality for the queer-looking little visitor whose hat was of such a fascinatingly mammoth outsize that, if some experimenting small-fry popped it on, it eclipsed him like a very small candle being snuffed by a huge extinguisher. As a clutch of children sat on his knees fondling the immense dome that had lately been covered by it, not an entrancing twitch, no doubt, of

Mr. Swinburne's person nor a rise and dip of the high, clear voice chanting to their parents escaped their pleased attention. When he visited their nursery, it was clear to them that he enjoyed being there more than in their mother's drawing-room, and the youngest Rossetti once suggested pressingly that he should stay indefinitely; an extra crib, she pointed out, could easily be slipped in between her cot and her sister's. Though he still took an affectionate interest in these young families as they grew older, the ecstasies grew markedly more restrained. Heaven lay about them in their infancies, and with the monstrous sprouting of their permanent teeth in their little mouths and the lengthening of their stout legs, the celestial light gradually faded.

Bertie Mason, Watts' nephew, the object of the prolonged antic of the heart which began in the first year or two of Swinburne's domicile at The Pines, was five years old when he came to live there with his parents, Mr. and Mrs. Charles Mason, so the dew of eternity had had time to dry on him. But 'of all children out of arms', Swinburne reported to his mother, he was 'the sweetest thing going at any price'. This celebrated and, indeed, very pathetic infatuation with a child, revealed so candidly and dolorously in 'A Dark Month', seems to show us, too, how much of the heart had been untenanted when the new obsession filled it. In the autobiographical verse-drama 'The Sisters', which he was to write in 1891, one of the characters, addressing Reggie Clavering, alias Algie Swinburne, hits the nail right on the head:

> Just a hot-head still—
> The very school-boy that I knew you first,
> On fire with admiration and with love
> Of someone or of something, always.

Swinburne still felt that youthful compulsion to worship

a human being or a cause, or both together. Ardour, keyed a shade too shrilly, for someone or something was a necessity, and his grateful affection for Watts, his devotion to the loving, anxious women down in Wiltshire, did not quite meet the bill. Then along came Bertie, filling the dusty hours at The Pines with an extraordinary new happiness. Part of the little boy's charm, engaging though he doubtless was, sprang from his being the closest as well as the sweetest thing going. He was under the same roof, a marvellously gay diversion in days of which the high spots of entertainment, the nearest thing to a good time, seem to be the morning bottle of ale and the evening readings aloud of Dickens. (For Dickens, a passion since his Eton days, when he used to wait eagerly for the monthly instalments of 'Bleak House', Swinburne's appetite was never glutted, though it may be that others at The Pines secretly shared Maarten Maarten's opinion of his reading style. When he had declaimed and chuckled his way from 'Pickwick Papers' to emerge at the other end of 'Edwin Drood', he began again after a three years' interval. The round trip was made, Watts calculated long afterwards, at least three times in the thirty years of domestic evenings watched over with a faint Olympian smile by Rossetti's chaste little Venus.)

But Bertie was better than Mrs. Gamp or Mr. Guppy or the Artful Dodger. He was alive, he said funny things, he presented Swinburne with 'a highly elaborate match-box, and a penholder which is also a pencil at the other end', he came to the door of the library and confidently demanded to be let in and shown books by his friend. Swinburne's immediate capitulation to Bertie has the eager concentration of a prisoner striking up an intimacy with a pet mouse. What was this pet child like? A photograph shows a sturdy, rather button-eyed small boy dressed in a knickerbocker suit, staring unsmilingly into the camera, one hand jauntily resting where his hip would be if he owned a ghost of one, the other dangling a round straw sailor hat. Beside him is stretched a canine door-mat, mouth open in a grin of indiscriminate affability, who one supposes is The Pines' guardian, Dido. The dog looks less overwhelmed than the boy by the ordeal of keeping still on the photographer's strip of carpet. Perhaps part of the mannikin's solemnity is caused by the awful responsibility of the best Sunday rig, the stiff collar, the uncomfortable-looking high buttoned shoes. Swinburne would have sympathized perfectly, for did he not, all his life, find anything starched against his sensitive skin a torture, and squirm like an electric eel if Watts persuaded him into a new suit, and refuse to sit to importuning artists and sculptors if he could possibly avoid the misery of remaining motionless for more than ten minutes?

That it was only a passing and unnatural expression for a boy who liked to laugh is clear from the fifty or so poems that Swinburne addressed to Bertie, as well as the anecdotes he relayed fondly to the Swinburne ladies and to receptive women friends—to Madame Dorian in Paris, for instance, who received regular reports over the years on 'Sa Majesté Herbert I' and translated some of the verses to show Victor Hugo. Bertie, he wrote to Mrs. Lynn Linton, was the 'brightest, bravest, quaintest of all his kind, and though "the gods have not made him poetical", they have given him a sense of humour which I never saw equalled at his age or perhaps at twice his age'. We hear Mrs. Linton rolling out some majestic sentiments on the friendship to Watts: 'Loving all children is pleasant, but loving one specially and doing what we can to mould the character and enrich the intellect is the greatest joy of middle life . . . when the passionate personality of our fervid youth has passed'. Watts seems to rumble something non-commital

89

and avuncular from the depths of the moustache. Nobody knew better than he did that the passionate personality of Swinburne's fervid youth was still to be reckoned with. The violence of the new attachment for his nephew was only another instance of that unfortunate tendency 'to *over do*'— as Lady Jane put it when they took anxious counsel together at the height of the tempest over Bertie—whether it was the emotions or the rush and pelt of words. 'Attachment' in the sense of being a new little human anchor which would help to keep Swinburne contentedly moored at Putney was, of course, excellent. He was endearingly like another child himself in the pleasure of introducing Bertie to Falstaff and Sam Weller, as his mother had introduced him at about the same age. The little boy rolled in rapture on the sofa; he could talk of nothing else but Sir John to his parents and uncle. Shrieks of laughter must often have floated down through the quiet house from the first floor back-room, perhaps making Hetty smile sympathetically as she grappled with another leg of mutton in the basement. Swinburne had one disappointment. Bertie's literal mind (would he be a scientist?) refused to believe in the woodcuts of the charming bird with its neck in a double slip-knot, and the mermaid carrying her tail in her hand like the train of a dress, and the other eccentric creatures with human faces that Swinburne showed him in the absolute pride, the choicest treasure in his library—an ancient 'black letter book' called *The noble lyfe and natures of man, of bestes serpentys fowles and fisshes yt be most knowen* by Lawrens Andrewe, which had been in his father's library at Holmwood and the joy of his own childhood. It was exhibited without fail to every privileged visitor over the years at The Pines. No, Bertie was *not* a poet. His eyes sparkled over the engravings of battles in Swinburne's Pictorial Shakespeare. Mars was plainly his guiding planet. He darted out into the road one day and hauled Dido gallantly out of the jaws of a large, aggressive Putney dog. He—but there was no end to the engaging doings and sayings of Bertie, some of which inspired poems that the cold world outside The Pines did not consider were particularly winged shafts of Apollo. The birthdays got a new poem each year from six to nine, when the natal verses stopped abruptly. A robust schoolboy does not encourage the muse, perhaps. Swinburne sometimes asked his friend, jokingly but with an undercurrent of real melancholy, if he could not stop the growing-up process and stay forever a child. One suspects that Swinburne himself would have liked that. His poetry is full of images of curling up and resting securely in some peaceful stable climate away from 'the ages of worldly weather', of hiding his soul in a place out of sight or his heart in a nest of roses.

But in 1881, and for a few happy years more, 'my little Bertie' or '*our* little boy' figures proudly in Swinburne's letters. In some odd but delightful way it is almost as though the sober partnership at The Pines has had issue. Had he not once been gratified to be told that a young woman admirer had resolutely refused to believe that A. C. Swinburne was a young man, since 'Atalanta' was so obviously the work of a mother who understood the pangs of maternity? Now, in middle life, he seemed to be enjoying a sort of phantom parenthood. He was working his 'best and hardest', finishing 'Mary Stuart', the manuscript of which had been lost several times and work on it abandoned in the old days of chaos in lodgings; there were also critical biographies of Landor and Marlowe to be delivered to the Encyclopædia Britannica. Bertie supplied a cheerful focus-point in the unvarying industrious routine. Just to think of the chattering child, asleep and silent at last in his little room, made Swinburne feel happy as he passed the door. He walked over to Wimbledon and came back with paper bags of crisp

gingerbread and currant biscuits stowed away in the large
poacher's pocket which he always had constructed in his
coats, to hold a volume or two or a rough draft of a poem
handily. Christmas in the bosom of dear Mimmie and Pino
and the girls used to bore him dreadfully in his youth—and
Easter, the season of 'Galilean orgies', he called it, was
worse—but now it was entirely different. Watts wrote one
of his ponderous poems about Christmas at The Pines some
years later, addressed to Swinburne, and it is clear that all
the ancient festive orgies were punctiliously celebrated from
the beginning.

> . . . And as to us, dear friend, the carols sung
> Are fresh as ever. Bright is yonder bough
> Of mistletoe as that which shone and swung
> When you and I and Friendship made a vow
> That childhood's Christmas still should seal each brow—
> Friendship's and yours and mine—and keep us young.

Swinburne, gazing with such amazing complacency at the
mistletoe bough, had already cheerfully described to his
mother Bertie's party on the Fifth of November, when
fireworks fizzed and spluttered in the back-garden. The
calendar was transformed. He was constantly preoccupied
with present-giving to the child, not only on birthdays. His
letters of these years to his publisher, Andrew Chatto, who
was also a book-seller, are full of strange requests: 'Dear Sir,
I shall be obliged if you will send me *Aunt Judy's Magazine*
for 1881 . . . Kate Greenaway's new 'birthday book' . . .
Mrs. Molesworth's new book "The Adventures of Herr
Baby", together with Mrs. Surr's "Stories about Cats",
which I see advertised as out . . .' He became a devoted
admirer, and soon a personal friend, of Mrs. Molesworth and
her tales for children. They corresponded warmly and
swapped stories of her younger son, Lionel, and 'the Vener-

able Bertie'. It disappointed Swinburne very much a few
years later when Mrs. Molesworth proposed dedicating her
latest work, 'Us: an Old-Fashioned Story', to Mr. Swinburne's little friend, and the Masons politely refused, in case
Bertie should be too set up by the compliment.

For the same reason, he was kept strictly in the dark
about the many poems Swinburne wrote to him. 'I flatter
myself', the poet told old Richard Henry Horne, the friend
of Elizabeth Barret Browning, 'no one child ever had so
many songs written in his honour'. Perhaps, a few years
later, school-fellows whispered and grinned, and the honour
became an affliction. Or perhaps he would grin back and
hardily not care, for he 'scorned all verses'. Meanwhile,
blissfully unconscious that 'To H. W. M.' would be in
printed books sold in Mr. Chatto's shop and lying on tables
in ladies' drawing-rooms, Bertie visited his friend daily.
They swung their four short legs companionably side by
side on the window-seat and bent their heads over the folios
Swinburne brought down happily from his shelves. One day,
he wrote his mother, they 'came upon the old woodcut
reproduced in so many books from some religious MS. of the
time of Edward III, representing a very fine young man
with curls and turned-up shoes, etc., meeting Death beside
an open grave at noonday face to face. Death is not a vulgar
skeleton, but a very lean, tall man partly draped with a
loose cloak thrown about him: very impressive, but not
disgusting or frightening'. Bertie wanted to know who the
tall man was. Swinburne told him. 'What is death?' Bertie
asked with interest. And at once another 'tiny poem' com-
busted, to be shown to Watts after dinner that evening.

Watts' bright, penetrating eyes no doubt regarded the
pair rather thoughtfully. It was the time when he had to
absent himself from The Pines for a night or two every
week, going backwards and forwards to Chelsea to cheer

Gabriel Rossetti. Each time he returned to Putney, he could see more clearly that Algernon's devotion to the little nephew was getting rather too emotional, as was Algernon's way. It would be no bad thing if he could take his mind off it for a while and work quietly without distraction. How fortunate, then, that Bertie happened to be going off on a visit for the whole of May—or was he sent away on purpose? It is not clear. At any rate, grasping an adult hand, Bertie climbs into a cab and is driven briskly away from The Pines.

The result of his departure was the very reverse of Watts' reasonable expectation. It was at once tragic and absurd. Swinburne seemed to lose his centre and spin like a demented top, faster and faster, emitting a shrill wailing note of anguish. Take his mind off it? Work quietly without distraction? His mind was nailed to the loss of his friend, and he was distracted. Stoicism, the keynote of the later years at The Pines, was abandoned; the gallant refusal to indulge in self-pity went sailing out into the road over the stone pine-apples. As for Nature, she seemed unable to exert her consoling power when he raced along the usual paths across the commons where the favourite hawthorn thickets were in flower. In this dreadful month of May she had no powers at all. Spring had suddenly become a death's-head winter, his gaunt hands full of 'cold cowslips' and his 'hoar grim head' crowned mockingly with a 'hawthorn bonnet'. The sun had been put out altogether, and when he walked out on a fine morning, the flowers jeered and leaves pointed scornful fingers, as Rossetti used to fancy crazily that the birds, trained by his enemies, were singing insults at him in the unkempt Cheyne Walk garden. The thirty-one days to fill before the silent house would come to life again seemed to Swinburne, a man of forty-four, a tract of time as vast as an adult's minutes and hours appeared to the reckoning of the smaller, slower child's timepiece in Bertie's own mind, or to

94

the even more creeping clock built-in under the wool of Dido the dog.

The thirty-one 'poems of lamentation' Swinburne wrote to tick off the dragging days make embarrassing but illuminating reading. The scholars, conducting us round the long out-of-fashion splendours of the collected works, all sheer off hastily from 'A Dark Month', muttering words like 'mawkish' and 'intolerable' as they reach for their hats. Yet the songs, even if they are not shafted by Apollo, tell us a lot about Swinburne. They tell, or blurt out miserably, too much. It is rather surprising that Watts, who was always so quick in suppressing the things he felt would be damaging to his friend's greatness, did not steal out one night when The Pines was sleeping and bury the lyrics to Bertie in the garden at the foot of Gabriel's gentle Venus, or cremate them in the kitchen stove with the methodical thoroughness which, later on, he so strangely did not apply to the combustible letters to Charles Augustus Howell. But he allowed them to survive, a piteous human lump, and to face the world. They appeared, chaperoned by the sturdy company of Swinburne's beloved Elizabethans in the sequence of 'Sonnets on English Dramatic Poets', in 'Tristram of Lyonesse and Other Poems' in 1882.

Perhaps the public eighty-eight years ago would have read 'A Dark Month' with approval as a sentimental but charming record of a poet's tenderness for a child, but when we read it now it seems merely melancholy. For the language in which Swinburne expresses his longing for a jolly little boy to hurry home and brighten up the place again with his funny sayings, his eager mind, and the gratifying warmth of his affection is horribly humble. One wonders why Sir Edmund Gosse's apologetic 'revelations' tacked on to the 'Life' were necessary when this sad little work says so plainly that Swinburne's essential dream is submission, and that it has remained basically the same. The implacable punishing women, the ruthless Madonnas of Pain, have simply been succeeded by a bullet-headed little boy in a knickerbocker suit—'my benevolent despot', as Swinburne affectionately called him. Now, writing in an extreme of bereavement that seems, like the woe of a child, to be able to see no end to the darkness, he laments the absence of his 'king' without whose firm rule 'my world is a cultureless island, my spirit a masterless slave'. The top spins giddily. We try not to notice its gyrations, yet it is impossible to avert the eyes from the spectacle of what happens to a son of Apollo when he no longer has all the universe to shoot over, but is cabined and confined in a semi-detached villa in Putney. Rachel mourning for her children was not more resolutely uncomforted than this top humming its tale of loss in the silence of The Pines. Is it, after all, thwarted parenthood which has lashed it into such a fury? And then we get confused and seem to be listening, not to a paternal voice, but to that of a lover bewailing a mistress who has left him and is probably faithless into the bargain, for Swinburne sharply accuses the seven-year-old child of having too good a time on holiday and not writing. Has he forgotten? Is it already 'out of sight, out of mind'?

> Not a ghost
> Of a word
> Riding post
> Have I heard
> Since the day
> When my king
> Took away
> With him spring.

Watts wrote anxiously to Lady Jane Swinburne. He himself was awkwardly caught, that spring of 1881, between the cross-fire of Gabriel Rossetti fast declining in Cheyne Walk, and of Swinburne, only too vigorously living and spinning and wailing at The Pines. Could Lady Jane perhaps write and drop a quiet hint to Algernon to calm down a little, not (in her phrase) 'to *over do*' in such an intemperate fashion this emotion for Bertie? Lady Jane returned a surprisingly firm reply. She feared it would be difficult to do so. A hint might check his happy openness on the subject, and if Watts and the Masons were worried that Algernon should 'inadvertently lead' Bertie into any harmful atheist views in the course of the two friends' chats on the window-seat, they would 'no doubt . . . guard the little child' from them. She was regretfully unable, too, to ask Algernon and Mr. Watts down to stay at Leigh House for a change of air and scene; the alterations to her new home were not yet complete; the carpenters and painters were in possession. She had 'only one spare room and small dressing-room and I am afraid you would not think it safe for him to come alone'. So with kind regards, dear Mr. Watts, she remained very truly his, Jane H. Swinburne.

The 'Dark Month' passed, in spite of everything. It must have been a slow and painful one for Watts, too, though for different reasons. For Swinburne, the anticipation of Bertie's homecoming became keen when it had got no further than the twenty-third day and song.

> The wind on the downs is bright
> As though from the sea:
> And morning and night
> Take comfort again with me. . .
> The sunset says to the moon,
> He is nearer to-night
> Whose coming in June
> Is looked for more than the light. . .

It would have been nice to observe the expression on the sensible intellectual face of Mrs. Lynn Linton, the purveyor

of the solemn remarks about the love of children being a
bonus when the passionate personality of our fervid youth
has passed, as she read this curious little document in due
course. For now we seem to be standing in the garden of
Mr. Tennyson's Hall, listening in muddled fashion to the
rooks in the high elms and to the young man waiting impatiently beneath the passion-flower dropping its tear at the
gate.

> The red rose cries, 'She is near, she is near;'
> And the white rose weeps, 'She is late.'

And late Bertie was. The pessimism of the white rose was
amply justified. June went by without him, and so did July.
August passed, and still Bertie was carefully banished to
some distant beach or relative's garden. Swinburne appears
to have accepted the disappointment with a return of his
dignified natural stoicism. He worked on 'Mary Stuart',
and corresponded animatedly with Mr. (later Sir) Sidney
Colvin in Cambridge over the study of Landor on which
Colvin was engaged. He went to see Benjamin Jowett
in Oxford, and was delighted by a visit of homage from
a total stranger, the distinguished French engraver, M.
Fortuné Méaulle, who turned up at The Pines to present
a proof set of his engravings of Victor Hugo's drawings of
the sea and the old streets of Guernsey. By the end of June,
indeed, he was so recovered that he was able to share with
his old friend, the painter William Bell Scott, his gleeful
discovery of a newspaper cutting which reported that a
printer called Matthew Arnold had been fined ten shillings
for playing tipcat in the streets with a couple of postmen
friends. (Swinburne childishly and happily crossed out
'printer' on the cutting and wrote 'poet', adding that it was
'the most scandalous example of genius degraded by eccen-
tricity' he had seen since the *Times* a few years back had

reported the arrest of a citizen called Robert Browning for running naked in Hyde Park one noon.) His spirits seemed to have bounded upwards in their cheerful Swinburnian way and thankfully left behind the sad, chilly cowslips, the glib *kings* and *springs*, *moons* and *Junes*.

When Bertie, sunburnt and merry, came stumping back at last in September, Swinburne wrote the exultant hosanna 'Sunrise', with which 'A Dark Month' ends. He explains, without details, how the household remaining at The Pines had 'trusted in June' to bring their child home, 'and by June been defrauded', and how 'joyless' July and then August, 'arid and sterile', went by also. But now all is well, and Nature begins to rustle, to beam, to deliver sweet sights and smells loyally as usual.

> For the days of the darkness of spirit are over for all of us
>     here, and the season
> When desire was a longing, and absence a thorn, and
>     rejoicing a word without reason.
> For the roof overhead of the pines is astir with delight as
>     of jubilant voices,
> And the floor underfoot of the bracken and heather alive
>     as a heart that rejoices. . .

because of the return of one small urchin in a knickerbocker suit. It seems to put the loneliness of Swinburne's life at The Pines, even with Watts, in rather awful perspective. The rapturous account of Bertie's homecoming that he must have sent off to his mother appears to have perished in the great bonfire of family letters made after the death of his cousin Mary, at her request. We can only imagine, unfortunately, how the roof of The Pines was also astir all that September day until wheels drew up at the gate; how Swinburne, a boy once more, flew joyfully down the stairs to welcome the travellers; and what a remarkable trade the Wimbledon pastry-cook did for the next few days in currant biscuits and gingerbread. Curiously enough, the happy ending of 'A Dark Month' seemed to end the exaggeration of the attachment, as though, by capitulating to it so completely, Swinburne had put himself beyond the conflict. Watts must have managed it all with immense patience and skill. For from now on, the tone is much calmer. We no longer have to ask our confused selves if this is an impatient lover standing under the passion-flower waiting for his life and his fate to shine out to the flowers and be their sun. Bertie was still the beloved child, but he was cheerfully referred to as 'The Seneschal', a title which suggests a comfortable joke about him running The Pines and everybody in it. As the years went by, *Aunt Judy's Magazine* gave way to *The Sea* and *The World of Adventure*, which Swinburne read avidly before passing them on to Bertie. The orders to Mr. Chatto were for strong stuff such as G. A. Henty's 'With Wolfe in Canada' and 'Harry Raymond, His Adventures among Pirates, Slavers, and Cannibals', by Commander Lovett-Cameron. Swinburne carried them upstairs and devoured them too. On Bertie's twelfth birthday, in 1886, he ordered Leech's 'Drawings from *Punch*' for him, or, as second choice, Scott's 'Waverley Novels' in half morocco binding, price twelve guineas—a handsome present from one of (as he described it himself) 'very narrowly limited income'. So Bertie vanishes from our sight, a nice, practical-minded schoolboy, towering over his little Uncle Walter and little Swinburne, still stoutly asserting that he 'wouldn't like to be a Shakespeare when he grows up', still showing signs of a scientific bent as befits a grandson of the old solicitor who once read a paper on luminous meteors to the St. Ives Society, and still fond of gingerbread from Wimbledon. Then there is a long gap, and when next he appears, it will be as Mr. Herbert Mason, a man of thirty-five, in the list of mourners at Swinburne's funeral, and we shall not recognize him.

## VII

THE METHODICAL round of life at The Pines, which
had been interrupted for a few months by the distracted humming of a top, returned to its placid
normal. Swinburne was to write many more poems celebrating or mourning his friends' children—he boasted to
Burne-Jones that he had 'discovered the one serious rhyme
in the language' to 'babe', which was, not very helpfully,
'astrolabe'—but he would never feel for any of them the
tenderness he had felt so intensely for Bertie. Perhaps the
queer emotional flare-up would not have happened at all if
Watts' attention had not been divided that year between
him and the old allegiance to Rossetti. Now that the sym-
pathy and the affection could all be concentrated on Swinburne, he became himself again—if we can decide which
self was the true one in the variety of bewildering beings
who at one time or another seemed to be uppermost in him.
He was soon busy seeing 'Tristram', with which 'A Dark
Month' was to be oddly yoked in the same volume, through
the press. For such an Argus-eyed, perfectionist reader of
proofs, it was always an exhausting, intensely exasperating
labour. Before each of his publications through the years, a
hail of small, sharp, stinging letters to Andrew Chatto
rattled out of The Pines as though blown from a pea-
shooter.

An extraordinary author-publisher relationship existed,
with both sides apparently understanding its rules perfectly,

between the charming, cultured, incredibly sweet-tempered Mr. Chatto, the successor to John Camden Hotten, who founded the firm of Chatto and Windus, and his valuable little property volcanically erupting from time to time on Putney Hill. When Swinburne took his pen in his hand to write a curt order to 74, Piccadilly (after 1880 the firm moved to Number 214) for books, or to point out that 'those predestinate sons of Tophet, the printers' (so he named them fumingly to Edmund Gosse) had once more misplaced a word or altered a comma in a poem, the daemon in charge was clearly the *grand seigneur* who liked to remember that he was descended from the noble French house of Polignac —a very tenuous link, as a matter of fact, but it was one of the romantic beliefs he cherished—and that the Swinburne family, Catholic until the nineteenth century and staunchly Jacobite, had always 'given their blood like water and their lands like dust to the Stuarts'. The tone to Mr. Chatto is lordly. How is it that something or other has not been done? 'You will remember it was my particular desire'—so off to the guard-room with 'the dog Chatto', as he sometimes called him to Watts. The sons of Tophet had turned 'Landor' into 'Larder'. Off with their heads! 'Dear Sir', he wrote crustily; only much later would he mellow gradually and occasionally into 'Dear Mr. Chatto'. 'Dear Sir . . . I have detected in the copy received this morning, blunders upon blunders, of the most scandalous kind, which would disgrace the lowest publishing house in London. I distinctly remember to have corrected some errors . . . and I perceive that these corrections have been impudently ignored, etc., etc.' One gets the impression that Mr. Chatto is a junior office boy suspected by the head of the firm of smoking in the stockroom. His photograph is of a trimly bearded gentleman with a broad, serene brow and a humorous twinkle in the eye. Serenity and humour he must have needed and possessed abundantly, with a capacity to soothe ruffled men of genius as softly skilful as Watts' own. Swinburne, in spite of his threats to change his publisher, remained with Chatto and Windus for life. His name proudly headed the anthology, 'A Century of Writers', with which the firm celebrated their centenary in 1955.

With 'Tristram' in print, the restless hunt for a new arrow to string to the bow began again. 'I rather want something big to do or at least attempt', he wrote to Churton Collins. Once more he was thinking of a subject for a historic tragedy which had been simmering in his mind quite as long as the theme of 'Tristram' had lain fallow. It had attracted him in 1861 when he was on a visit to Mentone, a resort on which even now, twenty-one years later, he heaped violent maledictions as 'a place which of all others upon earth . . . I most utterly abominate and abhor', recalling its 'exhausting nervous' climate and its everlasting backdrop of 'the dull metallic sapphire of a tideless pond'— so different, he added, from the sweet green *English* sea. The chauvinistic conviction, caught from Watts, that everything English is best, from beer to beaches, is already present. On that long distant, disenchanted visit he had cheered himself by writing in his favourite Sarah Gamp-ese nonsense to Lady Trevelyan, the intelligent older woman friend and adored confidante of his youth, that he was working on a story 'about my blessedest pet which her initials is Lucrezia Estense Borgia. Which soon I hope to see her hair is as kep at Milan in spirits in a bottle.' Now, a middle-aged man becalmed on the tideless pond of The Pines, he was drawn back to the old idea of a tragedy on the 'Holy Family' of the Borgias. All the same, he added to Collins, 'between triple incest and the bi-sexual harem of the Vicar of Christ—points which could not be wholly ignored in a chronicle history of the Borgias—even I feel conscious of

103

something like the sentiment called funk in face of the inevitable difficulties'. It was certainly far from rhymed yearnings for his blessedest pet Bertie; he managed the switch to fractricide and incest quite comfortably. The monstrous old dream could somehow nestle down side by side with humdrum, affectionate thoughts about gingerbread and *Aunt Judy's Magazine*. These bewildering divisions much distressed Sir Edmund Gosse when he was struggling with his 'Life of Swinburne'. How impossible it seemed to try to portray a character which had 'a very ugly side' and yet was so lovable! 'What humbug has been printed about his purity and high-mindedness!' he burst out to (of all people) the far from high-minded forger of Swinburne first editions, the then unsuspected and esteemed bibliographer, Thomas J. Wise. But the coin is spun again and down comes Apollo's head instead of the satyr's mask. Gosse adds the inevitable scrupulous, perplexed postscript: 'And yet, such is the paradox, he was pure and he was high-minded—on certain defined sides', he reflects in a still more cautious post-postscript.

The difficulties of tackling the Borgias, Swinburne found, were also impossible. He abandoned the tragedy and left it to glitter on alluringly, preserved in colourless fluid like the lock of Lucrezia Borgia's hair, until he took it out again when he was an old man. It was never finished. 'The Duke of Gandia', a fragment only of the grand chronicle he had planned, was published in 1908.

Meanwhile, Watts sat at his own untidy table in The Pines writing his regular articles and revising, over and over again, chapters of his tortoise of a novel 'Aylwin'. This long romantic work, full of gypsies and family curses and wild Welsh scenery, which interests impatient readers now, if at all, chiefly because Gabriel Rossetti figures in it portrayed as the painter D'Arcy, had been ready to put into the race as far back as 1874. No novel can ever have dawdled so long on its way to the circulating libraries, resting meditatively and then burying itself for years at a stretch. For some mysterious reason, Watts seemed loath to dig it up and push it out into the world. He appeared to desire to remain unknown. He had only recently begun to sign his literary essays, believing that 'anonymity was what especially suited my temperament'. Perhaps he feared criticism, to which he was painfully sensitive; a hostile comment on anything he had written would fill him with despair for days. Finally he was persuaded to have 'Aylwin' set up in page proofs in 1885, but only to have portions of it circulated among receptive friends. Lady Jane Swinburne and her daughters were allowed to read the first half in proof, and her breathless letter of thanks to Watts overflowed gratifyingly with praises. '. . . if you will forgive me I must tell you that I think it is the most wonderful and most clever story I ever read—its originality unflagging interestingness and though fearfully exciting the tone throughout is so entirely free from anything one could not quite like that I think it really a wonderful book.' Yet the tortoise still dallied and hibernated. It appeared at last in 1898, when Watts-Dunton (he had changed his name two years before) was sixty-six, and lo! promptly it became a hare! It raced off at mettlesome speed through the libraries; it ran into lush meadows of circulation and munched its way through seventeen editions in six months. Before Watts-Dunton died in 1914, the novel had been reprinted twenty-six times. It is now thoroughly forgotten, but then every novel reader in England, apparently, shared Lady Jane's views. Oscar Wilde pronounced it 'a capital book to give one's parents at Christmas.' It was, in short, an extraordinary success, and the delighted and startled author was emboldened into starting another romance. But this one remained a tortoise;

there was never a second hare to leap at a bound into the public's fancy.

The procrastination over 'Aylwin' was oddly typical of Watts. It is part of the unexpectedness of the man that he who was so shrewd, so firm and masterful in giving counsel and settling the muddled business affairs of his friends, should be diffuse and unmethodical in arranging his own work. He wrote prodigiously, eternally, but nothing much emerged. 'A great deal of work on hand just now—a great deal of work.' Thus he always greeted young Max Beerbohm arriving at The Pines, and Beerbohm used to 'wonder what work it was, for he published little enough'. Publishers stalked him hopefully, nevertheless. They wanted him to write a life of Dante Gabriel Rossetti. Who had known him better in the last years? Watts was always going to write a life of Rossetti, and then, after Algernon died, a life of Swinburne, but he died in his turn without putting pen to paper in memoriam of either cherished friend. Yet stacks of pens must have worn out, rivers of ink flowed, page after page was dropped on his favourite resting-place for all things, the floor, in the cosy, cluttered den where he sat furiously writing away. At what? Letters for much of the time, certainly. He conducted an enormous correspondence. The big mantelpiece looked as though some child had been trying his hand at building vast topless towers of letters, notes, invitations to dinner, which listed and tottered perilously along its length, until the fatal envelope was laid and the paper city collapsed into the fireplace. Watts answered them all, at great and time-consuming length. If a friend published a new poem or a new novel, or some totally unknown, struggling young writer forwarded a manuscript and asked for an opinion, off went a long, careful, and cheering letter. His enemies, gazing resentfully at the uncommunicative front door of The Pines, behind which lurked the double cordon of Watts or Mrs. Mason and a well-trained parlourmaid to keep them away from Swinburne, were apt to sneer at him as a cultivator of famous men only, a cheap-day tripper to Parnassus who would never have breathed its high and sparkling air at all if he had not arrived by hanging on for dear life to the coat-tails of the greater pilgrims. Yet many obscure, struggling men testified gratefully that he was always generously ready to help them with advice and, frequently, money.

So he sat writing away, and later, when the chronic short-sightedness of those deceptively bright eyes increased, dictating away to a secretary in a chaos of books and papers everywhere, on the floor, stacked high on chairs and tables. Later still, he had two secretaries to help with the great deal of mysterious work that was perennially on hand. And he read, or had read to him, seven newspapers a day. Plans for books, plots and characters on a vast scale were always churning about in his mind and then being abandoned. We seem to hear him, as Beerbohm heard him on that first visit to The Pines, richly booming in the distance enormous, rotund sentences that go on and on, but we cannot really catch the words across the space dividing us. Swinburne, with the extravagantly loyal enthusiasm he showed always for the work of his friends, pronounced Watts the greatest critic of the age. Yet what has survived from all these incessant labours, except our impression of a far-off voice rolling out elaborate phrase after phrase, page after stately dead page? The Muse of Literature, whom he served so devotedly, regretfully echoes her young Mr. Beerbohm and, yawning, murmurs 'Little enough'.

Now that Swinburne, isolated by his deafness, had accepted an increasingly home-bound existence at The Pines, Watts was able to go out and about once more, as in the happy days when he first came to London. Though

107

his watch and ward over his friend would never slacken—
indeed, the tactful guardian of the first few years at Putney
would become more possessive and careful as to who should
or should not be suffered to pass between the stone pine-
apples as time went on—he became again a familiar figure
at dinner parties and Academy *soirées* and first nights. Now
and then he met Bernard Shaw, the critic of the *Saturday
Review*, at the theatre. Shaw liked him and teased him.
Little Watts, he recalled years later, used to dye the tremendous moustache so outrageously that 'sometimes the
dye "crept" and blackened the stalls'. Perhaps it was partly
as material for his articles in the *Athenaeum* and the
*Nineteenth Century*, but Watts unfeignedly enjoyed the
company of the celebrated, and they often appeared to enjoy
his. So we see him lunching with Robert Browning and
staying with the Tennysons at 'heathery Aldworth', the
house the Laureate had built on a Sussex hilltop. He sees
much of the American minister, James Russell Lowell, and
goes often to visit George Meredith on Box Hill. 'Any day
you please to name', Meredith writes, 'and certainly you
will sleep here. Your coming will rejoice me. Give my
warm love to Swinburne.' 'You are indeed deep in the
Vortex of Dissipation!' Lady Jane exclaimed, a shade re-
provingly, when she came to London for a while in the
summer of 1889 and Watts had to make excuses of previous
engagements for not accompanying Algernon to see her. He
would tell E. V. Lucas when they met in the nineties that
at one time he 'dared not leave London' for fear that, if he
set foot outside the metropolis, he might miss some newly
arrived celebrity who was passing through. An avid appetite
for life was at the back of the mild tract of forehead, the
sharp squirrel eyes. Treed in The Pines, he must for a while
have given up a good deal of his collecting, hoarding, sampling of such congenial pleasures. But now he felt free to sally

out from Putney into the murmuring, fascinating thicket of literary London, where the great Victorian oaks still spread their shade majestically over all; from these excursions he brought back a store of news and fresh ideas for Swinburne. 'Watts tells me . . .' Swinburne would write, or 'I hear from Watts . . .' The last phrase can be read literally, for while much of the world had fallen silent for him, that resonant loud voice always reached him with ease. 'What does he say?' he would ask forlornly, turning to Watts at lunch when a guest with a less carrying voice was saying something he wanted to hear, and Watts would tell him. Watts had become, as it were, his interpreter, his leg-man, his proxy link with the city in which he had lived for nineteen years, on and off, without exhibiting the slightest affection for, or interest in, it and its citizens. He seemed, indeed, not to wish to see it again for more than a fleeting visit. London had slipped past like a dream in which only the dome of the British Museum Reading Room and a few houses of friends appear occasionally to solidify out of the blur, while East Dene and Northumberland remained crystal clear and bright to the end.

Though Swinburne had disappeared into Putney, many people still trained their telescopes attentively on the demure windows of The Pines. 'Well—shall I never see you again?' Robert Browning wrote sadly to him in 1881. Watts coming to lunch had been pleasant, no doubt, but one would be even more delighted to see Swinburne at one's table. The withdrawal and isolation became more pronounced every year. Whether Watts' 'desperate experiment' would have had such an extraordinary effect if Swinburne had not been afflicted with deafness is a teasing question. Nature having cast her vote for respectability, however, he hid in The Pines and would only be tempted out to dine where no alarming new faces and voices would be sprung on him—

with, for instance, his old friend and medical man, Dr. George Bird and his sister, Miss Alice Bird, in Welbeck Street. Dr. Bird was one of those links with the past to which Swinburne was always affectionately loyal. The Doctor as a young practitioner had attended on poor alcoholic Mrs. Leigh Hunt, and Sir John Swinburne, the adored grandfather, had been such an admirer and staunch friend of Leigh Hunt in his financial troubles that one of Hunt's sons was named 'Swinburne' in gratitude. It enraged the grandson that Dickens was supposed to have satirized Leigh Hunt (who was linked, oddly enough, to the end, for he died in a house in Putney High Street, not far from the future site of The Pines) in the sponging and rascally person of Harold Skimpole, and had defended himself against the absurdly libellous charge, as Swinburne wrathfully considered, with lamentable lameness.

And at Dr. Bird's table, he and Watts would often meet a very old friend—the sharp-tongued, brilliant old woman, Mrs. Procter, who was seemingly as immortal as his own Aunt Ju and herself a link, or a scintillating necklace of links, not only with Hunt, but with Charles and Mary Lamb, Coleridge, Wordsworth, Hazlitt, Blake, and Byron, who had been at Harrow with her late husband. She talked of them all constantly and wittily, without a trace of the inverted commas that people put round 'the dead', so that Swinburne felt 'as if one might and ought to call on them, or at least leave cards for them on the next landing'. Henry James, who found her splendidly amusing, was to write of her as the 'very interesting lady of extreme age' who would say 'You know William Hazlitt has fallen in love with such a very odd woman', as though it had happened last week, for 'death had beautifully passed out of her world'. It was an attitude Swinburne applauded. Mrs. Procter's gossip about Lamb—Lamb living and walking in and making a pun only, as it were, last Friday—would alone have been an instant passport to his affections. He and Watts were both what he called 'Lambolaters'. The front door of The Pines was thrown open to select fellow-worshippers who would be appreciative of one of the most treasured things in his library—Lamb's own interleaved copy of the poems of George Wither, in which the owner had pencilled copious comments. It was always a pleasure to Swinburne to find Mrs. Procter using her 'perilous tongue' almost without a pause in the Birds' drawing-room. It was never perilous to him. He would have liked to see her more often, but 'the old angel' lived in a flat in Westminster to which one had to go up in a lift, and a lift, he had admitted to Lord Houghton, 'is almost as impossible for my fancy to face as a balloon'. He, who had climbed Culver Cliff, could face the dizziest of natural heights with equanimity, but he drew the line, he said, at machinery.

Far closer and dearer friends, Richard Burton and his wife Isabel, were often guests at Doctor Bird's dinner parties when they were in England. They would turn up suddenly at The Pines from foreign parts, like a couple of darkly sunburnt sailors swarming ashore for an hour or two at some God-forsaken dull port, to sit smoking cigarettes and talking of old times in Swinburne's library. Rapturously delighted to see them, their host would bring out in their honour, naturally, his precious 'Black Letter Book'. It enchanted him to note that the great traveller was not so coldly sceptical of its fauna as Master Bertie Mason was apt to be. Such endearing human-faced birds and beasts might well exist somewhere, Burton gravely allowed, though he himself had never had the good fortune to come across them. Watts, if he padded in to join the party, would give a worried thought, no doubt, to the overwrought state in which Algernon was always left after one of 'Dick's' visits.

If he had dared, this might have been one of Swinburne's former friendships that he would have tried to suppress. Burton had been a far from admirable influence. Was there not some regrettable story of how he had once been seen, a huge figure striding out from, it may be, an evening at the dubious Cannibal Club, with his tiny, liquefied companion tucked tenderly under one arm, as though he were a spare bottle taken along to cheer the rest of the night? But Watts knew his man too well. Swinburne was 'courteous and affectionate and unsuspicious and faithful beyond most people to those he really loved' (it is Edward Burne-Jones who speaks). He would never, of course, be budged from his devotion to the friend with whom he had spent a magical holiday wandering happily among the gorges and waterfalls and haunted ruins of Auvergne in 1869. 'Auvergne, Auvergne, O wild and woeful land.' So he would begin his sorrowing 'Elegy' when Burton died in 1890. It contains some bitter stanzas aimed at Isabel who has become 'that poor liar, Lady Burton' in a furious letter to his dear Mrs. Lynn Linton. He was appalled by her destruction of her husband's manuscript of 'The Perfumed Garden' and by her 'popish mendacity' in having had Dick buried with the rites of her own Roman Catholic faith. But now, welcoming them to The Pines in the eighties, there was no shadow over his positively boyish joy at seeing both the Burtons, though we fancy we catch an expression, hard to define but not exactly joyous, flitting over those portions of Watts' face not eclipsed by the stupendous moustache, on the afternoons when, entering the house, he smelt a whiff of alien tobacco (he smoked himself and also, when Swinburne was safely resting, often enjoyed a whisky toddy) curling downstairs under the disdainfully flaring nostrils of Rossetti's 'stunners'.

The years went by, and the writing of elegies became

more frequent. It was comically ironic. Swinburne had so nearly died himself more than once. According to one of his favourite but not necessarily gospel legends, he had not been expected to live more than an hour after birth. Then he had narrowly escaped drowning, and his friends had thought that he was heading for an early grave in his riotous London days. Mazzini, who had mournfully expected 'his' young Poet to survive only a year or two, and Ruskin, with his fears that this beautiful rank growth of deadly nightshade would be stricken down in the full heat of its dazzling noonday, would have been astonished if they could have looked into the crystal ball and seen the healthy little man sitting among his books, fashioning memorial verses for friends who might have expected at one time to survive him. 'Your report of Algernon's health is most satisfactory', Lady Jane wrote thankfully to Watts, as though to her son's housemaster. And indeed it was. All the 'bilious attacks', the 'influenza' and the 'headaches' of the past had disappeared. When Swinburne was sixty-three he would complain of 'a shadowy touch' of lumbago, but he could always manage to walk the pain away, drive it off, characteristically, 'by bullying it with exercise'. His sight, as though to make up for his deafness, was excellent, and his little red-veined aquiline nose was like 'a bloodhound's', he boasted, '. . . for all sweet smells—and alas! for all other than sweet'. Had not this sensitive organ once in his youth nearly doomed him to a poisoned death out of a Renaissance tragedy by imbibing the scent of an Eastern lily placed in his bedroom so recklessly that he sickened with a fever? He slept soundly now in his narrow, monastic bed, in contrast to Watts, whose placid countenance concealed a raging insomnia, and who averaged four hours nightly before rising to make his tea and, soon afterwards, to plunge resolutely into that ocean of important work. Swinburne never felt so well, it was true, when he was away from The Pines, but a cold now and then was the extent of his ailments for many years. He was growing quite plump. There he sat in his room, which smelt pleasantly of old leather and was increasingly cluttered in its lower shelves with the stout packages in which he seems to have bundled up every scrap of paper on his table from time to time—manuscripts, letters, bills, proofs, catalogues —until the day of his own death. Perhaps the Howell letters vanished somewhere in the vast accumulation. He and Watts were both dug in behind a great mass of paper, snug as a couple of silver-fish. There he sat, transformed into a surprisingly robust little ageing man, writing elegy after elegy to friends who dropped away silently through the years.

There are no less than three grieving poems in memory of George Powell, who died unexpectedly six months after Gabriel Rossetti in 1882. He was a friend of Swinburne's own generation. In mourning him, he was finally saying good-bye, too, to the brilliant being, Algernon Charles Swinburne, who had passed away in 1879, for every death of a friend of one's youth is a death to oneself. Powell had known and loved him without reserves of any kind, accepting the noble side and the ugly that so baffled the genteel imagination of Edmund Gosse. Their friendship had apparently begun (though they had both been at Eton) through a letter of fervent admiration Powell wrote after the publication of 'Atalanta'. Swinburne's many letters to Powell over the years were all carefully kept and flatteringly bound up in small leather volumes, which Powell promised to keep out of the sight of the Philistines. In spite of the promise, the thought of his spirited scrawls being respectably stabled in this way probably slowed down Swinburne's wild gallop occasionally to a more decorous pace. Powell was a wealthy, amiable Welsh landowner who had inherited a ghostly old mansion, Nant Eos, in some of the loveliest country in Wales, where he spent as little time as possible; he could not endure polite county society. Swinburne stayed with him there, and also at Étretat that summer when the fishermen hooked him up out of the sea and thus preserved him for The Pines. Young Guy de Maupassant, another summer visitor, had made the acquaintance of the rash swimmer and his friend. Years later he passed on to Henry James a confused impression of the Englishman's eccentric household, which had included a supernaturally intelligent pet monkey called Nip, and of Swinburne's strangeness and charm. Swinburne must have thought of Étretat often as he sat in Putney, happy, as he constantly averred, but with a very different kind of happiness, writing 'A Dead Friend'. In the pre-Watts days, Powell had been untiring in executing all the imperious commissions showering in on him in London when Swinburne was recovering from another alcoholic 'bilious attack' with his family in the country. The good-natured man would patiently arrange for journals and books to be posted, interview landladies, send carpets to be cleaned, look for the everlastingly mislaid belongings, and settle the bills of dunning tradesmen for his friend. If there had not been a Watts, it would clearly have been necessary to invent one. So strong, to some natures, was the attraction of Swinburne's total worldly helplessness that an obliging Powell would always have stepped into the vacuum.

The death of such a staunch old friend was a heavy blow to Swinburne. He heard the news when he was paying his autumn visit to Lady Jane at Leigh House. 'However, it is no use wailing', he wrote to Watts, adding in Greek: 'Being mortals, we have suffered'. His fancy continued to dwell mournfully on 'poor dear George'. Powell had been passionately devoted to music, a pleasure which he tried to share with Swinburne. It is doubtful if he really succeeded. Swinburne's superb ear for poetic metre was curiously deaf, even before actual silence closed down, to music. Once, a lady invited him to listen to a very ancient little Florentine air that some scholar had only just discovered. Solemnly she sat down at the piano and played 'Three Blind Mice'. Swinburne was ravished. He said that it captured perfectly 'the cruel beauty of the Medicis'. But Powell had been one of the ardent early enthusiasts who helped to make Wagner fashionable in London, and Swinburne caught a little of the excitement. Now, three months after Powell's death, his adored master, Wagner, died. Could it be, Swinburne wrote to his sister Isabel, that George 'had gone before to announce his [Wagner's] coming?' The thought, so uncharacteristic of him, was doubtless read out approvingly over the feminine breakfast table at Leigh House. He used it in one of his poems to Powell. He was as fiercely antitheist as ever, but a few questions about the possibility of some sort of personal immortality, perhaps influenced by Watts, occur wistfully from now on in the poems and letters, as in 'Past Days', a reverie on the happy Étretat holiday.

> Bound am I with time as with a tether;
> Thee perchance death leads enfranchised on,
> Far from deathlike life and changeful weather,
> Dead and gone.

Far, too, from the Swinburne who wrote proudly that:

> We thank with brief thanksgiving
> Whatever gods may be
> That no life lives for ever;
> That dead men rise up never;
> That even the weariest river
> Winds somewhere safe to sea.

Dead men rose up, he noted, and walked with remarkable

vividness through his dreams. He dreamt sometimes of his father, the Admiral, and of the favourite red-haired sister who had died young. Dear Pino and Edith returned to him as he lay asleep at The Pines, where neither of them had ever set foot, and they all talked and laughed with so much delightful naturalness that he remembered the conversations later as clearly as though they had actually happened. He was convinced, he wrote to his mother in 1885, that death does not really separate people. The 'insuperable and irremediable separation' was caused by the ultimate sin of unworthiness to a friend, or a friend's betrayal of oneself, in life. Then their voices fell silent, their faces became indistinct, they withdrew sadly and hopelessly into the shadows. He was thinking, as usual, of Rossetti, 'the friend who died to me—by his own act and wish', he had called him. The nagging pain of that insuperable separation thirteen years ago from the only true fellow-spirit he had ever known would never let up.

Powell's death, as a matter of fact, must have saved a good deal of awkwardness. Watts' apprehensive mind would certainly have filed this early friendship of Algernon's in the brimming 'Undesirable' pigeonhole. It is unlikely that he would have been encouraged to become a frequent visitor to The Pines, and it is hard to picture him there. He looks rather too life-sized, too careless and cheerfully amoral an inhabitant of a different world, to settle well among the antimacassars in the plebeian odours of roast mutton. He had always been on cordial terms with Watts, careful to write to him for news of 'our dear Bard' and to stake no tactless possessive claim of earlier friendship, and yet . . . And yet it seems probable that before long 'poor dear George' would have been dropped as quietly, as prudently, as Swinburne appears to have shed other chapters of his past after the move to Putney. However that may be, a rather touching

117

link with Powell that Swinburne had brought along with his few belongings remained carefully preserved at The Pines until his death. In a corner of the little box-room up in the tower, the coquettish toque crowning the sedate visage of The Pines, was a trunk containing the coarse sacking blouse and trousers in which the men on the French fishing-smack had dressed their tiny, half-drowned English fish when they landed him off Étretat in 1868. ' My sea-breeches', Swinburne called the rig-out. 'Give my love to my fishermen', he wrote to Powell when his friend was paying another visit to the Étretat cottage. It had been one of the key experiences of his life, and he often harked back to it.

In 1886, when he was forty-nine, Swinburne wrote the touching lyric that purposes to be a poem addressed to a seamew and is in reality an elegy for himself. It was a particular seamew that he singled out from the multitude shuttling up and down the towering cliff-face of Beachy Head. He and Watts were taking their September holiday in lodgings on the less populous outskirts of Eastbourne, and Bertie, now a twelve-year-old schoolboy, was there, too, for some of the time. The weather was good; they managed to swim a good deal. The conditions do not seem right for a sudden passionate cry of longing to escape; to catch a train anywhere without having somebody find out whether it was a safe, dependable slow or not; to leave Bertie and Walter in 197, Seaside Road and to swim out to sea, perhaps, until the coast of England, with The Pines seeming to stand tiptoe and wave farewell from the top of Beachy Head like an immensely respectable Hero bidding adieu to her Leander, faded from sight. Some such confession of intent startles us in the poem, for Swinburne has gone out of his way from time to time to insist that he is perfectly contented with his lot and would not have it otherwise. He had spoken scornfully, in a letter to his mother, of those people who go on and on about youth being the happiest time of life. What stuff they talked! 'Thank God ... I am very much more than twice as happy now as I was when half my present age just twenty-four years ago.' Could anything be plainer and more gratifying to Watts than that, if indeed a son of Apollo wants or needs happiness as lesser mortals do? The poem is responsible for reviving the tiresome spirit of doubtfulness that refuses to allow George Powell to make himself genially at home on the Chinese smoking divan and rattle away under the heavy-lidded gaze of Mrs. William Morris. Would it, after all, have been accounted a better thing for poetry, in the ledger where such things are totted up, if Watts had fallen ill, taken fright, gone back to St. Ives and become editor of a local journal, or in any way we like to imagine had not been on hand to save Swinburne from dying in the mess and confusion of Guildford Street? Some say one thing and some another. The balance sheet will always be argued over.

For it seems certain that during these years before the dust settles thicker on The Pines, everything gets shabbier and looks smaller, and Swinburne and Watts turn finally into the well-known Dickensian old buffers in carpet slippers who stand debating a literary point, or maybe coming to rest together in tired familiarity without words, in Max's drawing, there are moments of acute depression. The poem to the seamew tells us about them. In the middle of the happy domestic holiday with the two people he loves best in the world besides his mother and sisters, Swinburne suddenly addresses the seamew with intolerable longing and envy.

> When I had wings, my brother,
> Such wings were mine as thine:
> Such life my heart remembers

> In all as wild Septembers
> As this when life seems other,
> Though sweet, than once was mine;
> When I had wings, my brother,
> Such wings were mine as thine.

But they had not been so powerful as those marvellous free-wheeling pinions. Some essential quill or dynamic necessary for them to soar safely in storm or calm was missing.

> We are fallen, even we, whose passion
> On earth is nearest thine;
> Who sing, and cease from flying,
> Who live, and dream of dying;
> Grey time, in time's grey fashion,
> Bids wingless creatures pine:
> We are fallen, even we, whose passion
> On earth is nearest thine. . .
>
> Ah, well were I for ever,
> Wouldst thou change lives with me,
> And take my song's wild honey,
> And give me back thy sunny
> Wide eyes that weary never,
> And wings that search the sea;
> Ah, well were I for ever,
> Wouldst thou change lives with me.

Soon after that the party returned to Putney, and the gate of The Pines shut, gently but firmly, for another twenty-three years.

# VIII

'I WAS born in what is called the aristocratic class—an accident which I share with Byron and Shelley, the only two other English poets brought forth in these later generations who have had faith in republican progress and freedom ... At an early age, without teaching or example, I became convinced of the truth and justice of the republican principle, and I have always looked to the land of Dante and Mazzini ... to take the lead in realizing that idea for Europe.'

Swinburne had written this statement of belief in 1872 in a letter to a scholarly Italian admirer, Giuseppe Chiarini. Mazzini, 'the man whom I most loved and honoured of all men on earth', had died that year. The cause of Italian unity, the passionate enthusiasm of Swinburne's youth and inspiration of 'Songs Before Sunrise', was won by then. Italy could no longer fire poetry, but more than a decade and a move to Putney later, he still reserved for her the unique place of the first and best loved. He was filled with excitement when Aurelio Saffi, Mazzini's friend and the only surviving member of the triumvirate of the Roman Revolution in 1849, came to tea one May afternoon in 1884 at The Pines. Saffi had been Swinburne's Italian professor at Oxford when he was living in exile in the fifties; his pupil had gratifyingly carried off the Taylorian Scholarship for Italian and French in his second year. He called on Swinburne and Watts on his way back from Edinburgh, where he had gone to receive a degree. It was a gala occasion. Saffi was now sixty-five, but except for being slightly grizzled round the temples, Swinburne thought affectionately that he had hardly changed at all. The host ran up and down his library ladder, bringing out his finest Renaissance bindings and types, and happily pointing out their beauties to Saffi. Bertie, kept back from his favourite amusement of going fishing in the ponds on the common and forced, doubtless, into the fearful regalia of Sunday and his solemn face, came in to make his bow to the illustrious visitor, while Swinburne beamed and his mother and Uncle Walter looked on proudly. Did the little boy really know anything about the Roman Revolution? Saffi, looking pleased and amused, asked the question. 'I think you may trust *me* for that', said Swinburne simply. And indeed Saffi might. The window-seat sessions may not have imparted to Bertie any antitheist notions, as Lady Jane had thought alarmingly possible, but they had certainly opened the gate into a Child's Garden of Republican Principles. Mazzini and Victor Hugo, King Bomba and the hated Louis Bonaparte, whom Swinburne had still pursued with inexorable curses six months after his death, wandered down its paths in company with Sam Weller, Sir John Falstaff, and Richard Crookback. After all, had not Swinburne once thought of himself as practically an honorary Italian? He had said 'we' one day in talking to Mazzini, and when he flushed and apologized, his Chief had put him in the seventh heaven by saying kindly that he did not know anyone with a better right to call himself an Italian if he liked. In his usual fashion, he had lost all interest abruptly in Italy's future as soon as the battle was won. He never had any curiosity about what happened next; the young men who would follow, in poetry or in politics, remained faceless phantoms compared with the brilliantly lit places and great figures on which he had fixed his devotion in his youth. Yet he was pleased by every sign that Italy had not, in her turn, forgotten Mazzini's poet. Though he had vanished from sight into The Pines, his name was immediately proposed, and accepted with enthusiastic applause, as a member of a national committee to raise funds for a monument to be erected in Viareggio to the memory of Shelley. A few years later, an Italian senator paid an eloquent tribute in Parliament to Swinburne's long friendship with Italy. He was deeply touched.

As the years passed in Putney and world events rolled over the villa on the Hill rather as the procession of storm clouds roll over the blasted heath in 'Lear', realistically thunderous but comfortably remote from a real tempest to the watchers in the audience, very odd things happened to some of Swinburne's loves and hates. He was deeply interested in current affairs, but his impression of them came from the papers or were shaped in the ceaseless dialogue with Watts, also a keen student of politics. He was much as a man might be to-day who, at the age of forty-two, was sat down in front of a television set and told to gather all his ideas from that in future. Though he was informed about what was going on, there were huge gaps in the picture which could only have been filled in if he had smashed the set one day, fetched his wide felt hat from the end of the hall, and shaken the dust of Putney forever off his little boots. It might have been enlarged if he had been able to hear some spontaneous opinions from ordinary people met through casual encounters, but nothing in his life was casual. Nobody—except perhaps the Burtons, who made their own rules—dropped in at The Pines. The somebodys who were invited there came for a specified purpose, and they were always cautioned by Watts to be punctual, for to be kept waiting upset the Bard. His quiet hours were charted so precisely that the slightest deviation altered their balance. Unscripted outside meetings were unthinkable. He talked to nobody on his walks, apparently, except to Mrs. Frost, the gentle Jane Austen lady who kept the bookseller's and stationer's shop in Wimbledon High Street and was a friend, and of course to any child who trundled a hoop or chased a kite across his path. 'Look', a mother or a nurse-maid would command, 'there goes Mr. Swinburne', and some of the children looked and remembered the strange little fleeting figure all their lives. But his defective ears made the everyday world of humour and coarse common-sense stand off at a distance and become dumb as an oyster. In the silence, everything except literature tended to turn ingrowing and sometimes to become enlarged out of propor-tion, as the fondness for a little boy had developed into something manic.

Some of the postures Swinburne took up towards the nation's affairs during the Putney years seem indeed as giddy as his spinning and wailing over Bertie Mason. Old friends suddenly became foes, and old foes were castigated with redoubled ferocity. The firebird veered like a weather-cock, swung round by gusts of violent feeling, now pointing his golden arrow to the republican clime of his youth, now turning sharply away to the loyal and temperate zone of Putney, and sometimes trying to face both ways at once when watchers from far off pointed out acidly that the wind had certainly changed.

The poems Swinburne wrote on political topics during the eighties and the nineties were often as disconcerting to his admirers as they are mostly unreadable to us now. They doubtless read better at the time when Watts bore them off, sizzling hot, to the editors. Frequently they embarrassed and alarmed Watts, who did his utmost to suppress them. He failed very often. The theory put about by some of Swin-burne's resentful friends that Watts had an infallible mesmeric power over him breaks down awkwardly. Though he could soothe and adroitly suggest a train of ideas that Swinburne, nine times out of ten, would follow with child-like docility, Watts knew perfectly well that when the child was bent on some headstrong course, no voice on earth could stop him. He was, unfortunately, completely without thought for his own interests. It must often have occurred to Watts, lying awake in the night listening to The Pines talking quietly to herself and mentally shuffling around a comma or two in a proof-sheet of 'Aylwin', that one day someone would have to be appointed to succeed his dear and revered Tennyson as Poet Laureate. It was discouragingly true that Swinburne had a sturdy radical aversion to any honours more worldly than an occasional tribute in the Italian Parliament. As a matter of fact, he was fond of rapping out the scornful invocation 'May I die a Poet Laureate!'—the awful fate he wished on himself if he failed to do something or other. He raged when Tennyson accepted a peerage in 1883 and the Tory press made obsequious remarks about the great man's elevation to the House of Lords. The rage overflowed into the heavily sarcastic poem 'Vos Deos Laudamus'. 'Stoop, Chaucer, stoop, Keats, Shelley, Burns, bow down: These have no part with you, O Lords our Gods'.

The peers were a favourite target. A year later, angered further by what he considered the pusillanimous hesitancy of the Upper House, Swinburne haughtily advised it to dissolve itself forthwith and get out. The lineal descendant of Hotspur (as he claimed himself) reminded their Lordships that some of them could only be addressed as Their

> Graces by grace of such mothers
> As brightened the bed of King Charles.

The lines have a neat Gilbertian ring. The comparison

would not have displeased him. He was a keen admirer of
'The Bab Ballads' and the comic operas.

> Bright sons of sublime prostitution,
> You are made of the mire of the street
> Where your grandmothers walked in pollution
> Till a coronet shone at their feet.

It was not the way, as understood by sober citizens in St.
Ives, Huntingdonshire, to address a duke. It was no way,
certainly, to ingratiate oneself in the highest quarters, but
then Swinburne had never dreamt of ingratiating himself
with anyone in his life. Watts may have shuddered, but 'A
Word For The Country' was snapped up by the radical *Pall
Mall Gazette*. The country ignored it comfortably. The House
of Lords remained intact. If the cards were played carefully
in future, it was possible that all this could be forgotten.

So we seem to hear a steady domestic hum, somewhat
like the cosy singing of a kettle, floating out of the room at
The Pines where the two friends sit talking. It is Watts
suggesting, Watts praising, Watts giving sage reasons to
Algernon for following up the old fervent hymns to the
sunrise of European republicanism with new songs lauding
the apparently never-setting imperial sun beaming on the
possessions of Queen Victoria. He did it marvellously well.
For suddenly Swinburne, the joyous celebrant of the breasts
of the nymph in the brake, began to reel out yards of
serviceable red-white-and-blue flannel made in England.
The noble and nude and antique, or large violet-eyed goddesses called Italy or Humanity or simply Right, had always
been necessary to move him to warble songs of ecstasy or
indignation. Now they were succeeded by the most beautiful
of all—Britannia on her penny, ringed round by her cold
bracing seas. He was 'on fire with admiration and with love'
again, this time of a bigger 'something' than little Bertie
Mason.

In 1887, England was in the grip of Golden Jubilee fever. Swinburne might have been expected to stay aloof from all the loyal jollifications planned to celebrate the fiftieth anniversary of the Queen who had come to the throne in the year he was born. His private references to Victoria had never been as exquisitely courteous as his manners to women invariably were—far from it—and the thought of stepping out a half century with her would not, we might feel, have stirred him. All his golden dates were republican ones. He had once fondly twitted Lady Jane for her really deplorable bad management in giving birth to his brother Edward on July 14th, the anniversary of the fall of the Bastille, instead of to him. Or could they possibly have got their birthdays muddled in the nursery? The one monarch for whom he always romantically threw over his Mazzinian principles of faith wholesale was Mary Stuart, the 'Queen for whose house my fathers fought', the never dimmed 'Red star of boyhood's fiery thought'. Even so, he added a republican footnote. He sometimes expounded an ingenious theory that if the English had succeeded in restoring the Stuarts and driving out 'the Hanover rats', the country would only have stood twenty or thirty years of Stuart rule, and then— and then would have surely come the dawn of the glorious Commonwealth of England, without the puritanism and militarism which had brought it down after Cromwell's death. Perhaps it would actually turn out to be a greater affair still. Looking into the vision of the future with his poet's eye, he had predicted as far back as 1877: 'We shall none of us live to see "The United States of Europe" (Victor Hugo's great prophetic phrase) but . . . other and happier men will "in some diviner day" '.

Only a few years before the Jubilee, indeed, Swinburne had written a hilarious letter to Georgiana Burne-Jones, solemnly asking her if she had heard of a tragic drama which was about to be given in Paris. It has been founded, he says, on Her Majesty's new volume of 'Leaves from the Journal of Life in the Highlands', with its dedication to the memory of her loyal departed Highlander servant, John Brown. Its title is *Sir Brown: drame en 7 actes et 49 tableaux.* To Ned Burne-Jones, chuckling over the extracts passed on to him from this spirited work, it must have brought back wonderfully the little Swinburne of their youth, whose tearing spirits had rattled off the other burlesque French dramas of the sensational intrigues going on behind the scenes at Buckingham Palace, *La Fille du Policeman* and *La Soeur de la Reine.* In the latter extravaganza, Queen Victoria lives a scandalous sex life and has the headmaster of Eton executed for tactlessly mentioning Messalina to his pupils. (After Swinburne's death, Edmund Gosse poured a cold bath of derisive scorn on Thomas J. Wise's ingenuous suggestion that it might be nice if these works were translated.) As in the earlier parodies, the tiny fragment of *Sir Brown* Swinburne composes for Mrs. Burne-Jones' amusement is supposedly written by a French author with a very imperfect knowledge of English history, place names, and titles, all of which he scrambles recklessly. Queen Victoria is discovered at *Osborne's House, Ile de Wigth*, impatiently waiting to hear from her lover Brown that he has succeeded in doing away with the Prince Consort. Sure enough, *Entre Brown. Grand costume de Higlander.* When the Queen enquires anxiously *C'est fini?* he is able to reply, *Tu l'as dit. Mais embrasse-moi donc aussi, toi, ma reine!* Falling into his arms, Victoria cries, *Mon Johnny! Mon Jack adoré! Je vais donc enfin être toute à toi!* At the end, imperial vice does not triumph. Swinburne briefly, and with relish, outlines the final stunning curtain. The Prince of Wales, escaped from imprisonment in the Tower of London, stabs Brown to the heart at the feet of the Queen, exclaiming like a stout Hamlet to the restless paternal shade, *Dors en paix, ô mon père! Tu m'avais donné la vie—je te donne la vengeance!* The Burne-Jones greatly enjoyed the nonsense, but one suspects that this may have been a letter that Swinburne did not read aloud to Watts.

His reactions to Victoria's Jubilee, however, were all, or nearly all, that could be desired. He was caught up in the wave of patriotic emotion that swept through the household at The Pines and every household in England. The excitement was contagious. Swinburne wrote to Andrew Chatto, asking if the publisher could find seats in his corner windows in Piccadilly for three friends—Watts, Miss Theresa Watts, and Bertie—to watch the Queen drive in state to Westminster Abbey for a Jubilee Thanksgiving service on June 21st. For himself, he and Watts thought of 'running down—and up—to Beachy Head', the home of his seamew, in the evening to see the bonfire lit there—one of the chain of loyal beacons that ringed the coast with fire that night from John o' Groats to Land's End. He wrote to his sister Abba chiding her for planning to be out of England—in Germany, too!—on the great day. How could she think of missing it? He was delighted that she liked his ode, 'The Jubilee' in the June *Nineteenth Century*. (It was later published in 'Poems and Ballads: Third Series', re-titled 'The Commonweal'.) Watts had come home this very minute, he added, bringing with him a bit of news that would amaze Abba. He had just heard that the ode had been warmly admired by—who did Abba think? The Prince of Wales! Swinburne pretended to be as surprised by this as if he had learnt that the Queen herself and Mr. Gladstone, whom he detested and often attacked bitterly in verse, had liked it. He insisted that its fifty stanzas, one for each year of the reign, were as essentially republican in spirit and tone as anything he ever wrote, though it is difficult for us to see it as a bugle call to the barricades. It offered brief and graceful homage, naturally, to 'a blameless queen', but Watts had urged him to say a good bit more about Victoria. It had been one of the times when he had not listened to Watts. He was plainly delighted, all the same, that the Prince of Wales had approved of the ode.

And Watts, we may feel, was also well content. It was a fine, stirring piece of work. It had caught the royal eye, not much given to the rapturous reading of poetry. A mood of comfortable congratulation succeeded the excitement. 'How more than satisfactorily the good Queen's Jubilee has gone off!' Swinburne wrote to his mother a few days later, in somewhat startling republican vein. He seems to have adopted the ageing Queen as an object of tenderness and veneration, almost as though she were a particularly durable member of his own family like his grandfather or his tough, indomitable Aunt Ju. Her Jubilee had been a blaze of excitement in the dull routine of The Pines. Bertie had rushed up to his friend's library, the moment he and his aunt and uncle got back from Piccadilly, and had poured out ecstatic descriptions of the splendours of the procession— the uniforms, the horses, the romantic potentates, white or black or brown-skinned, who had travelled to London to advertise to the world how vast and various was the Empire of the Great White Queen. They could not have had better seats or a finer view anywhere on the route, Watts added when he followed Bertie upstairs. Swinburne was so gratified that he wrote a note of thanks that evening, actually beginning 'Dear Mr. Chatto'. He and Watts both thought, he told Lady Jane down in Wiltshire, that the 'genuine and really beautiful success [of the Jubilee] . . . will have been . . . a heavy blow to the enemies of England'.

\* \* \*

Swinburne became increasingly preoccupied with the enemies of England as he grew older. Through the years, a stream of intensely patriotic topical poems, the worst really little better than rhymed journalese, came tumbling out of The Pines in a truly Laureate-like flow. They proved in the most satisfactory way that Mr. Swinburne's muse was as ready as Lord Tennyson's to hymn a national occasion. Watts thankfully found a ready sale for the ones he did not consider too dangerously vituperative to get into print; we have to wish that he had managed to suppress more. The generation of young men to whom Swinburne had always stood splendidly for revolt read them with dismay. It seemed unbelievable to them that he had swerved from the libertarian views of his youth to this truculent chauvinism, to have 'passed', as was bitterly said, 'from the van to the rear-guard, forsaking the Ayes for the Noes'. It was as disconcerting as though some leading student radical to-day should suddenly be observed to have quitted the streets and to be settled comfortably in an armchair in the window of a St. James's club, reading *The Times*. Swinburne denied the charges scornfully. He was fond of quoting William Blake's pronouncement in 'The Marriage of Heaven and Hell' that a man who never changes his opinions is a stagnant water and breeds reptiles of the mind. But opinions, he would add, were not to be confused with principles. His own principles still stood like rocks. He found no difficulty in reconciling the doctrines of republican liberty with affectionate appreciation of Queen Victoria and furious denunciation of any of her rebellious subjects who were ungentlemanly enough to wish to rule themselves.

One attitude of his youth, indeed, never suffered a sea-change in the warm aquarium fluid of The Pines through the years that we continue to observe Swinburne and Watts (soon the label on the tank will be changed to read Watts-Dunton) seated side by side, like a couple of hermit crabs of indefinite antiquity, motionless in their dark grotto. A solid rock in the tableau was Swinburne's implacable hatred of the rulers of Russia. Like everything lasting in his life, it had started early; it dated from his boyhood emotion when the news of Balaklava reached the family at East Dene. In 1880, Czar Alexander II's splendid new yacht, the *Livadia*, was launched, and Swinburne called down his most blistering imprecations to speed the vessel and her imperial passengers on her way.

> All curses be about her, and all ill
> Go with her. . .

Death, he prayed, should be their compass, and despair their star, until 'the white foam [made] a shroud for the white Czar'. The gods answered almost immediately. Alexander II was assassinated by a Nihilist bomb in March the following year. Swinburne was exultant. 'At last!' he wrote triumphantly to William Rossetti, ' "One more unfortunate" has joined *quel cattivo coro' di re'*—Dante's 'caitiff choir of kings'. The brutal crushing of the Polish patriots' rising in 1863 was paid for, and he felt 'at peace with all or most men, and ready to make allowances for God'. He could be sure there of a sympathetic audience, but Watts nervously counselled a little restraint in proclaiming further jubilation in public. Queen Victoria's son Prince Alfred, Duke of Edinburgh, had married the dead Czar's daughter Marie. The plump hand of the monarch was busy recording in her journal her 'ineffable thrill of horror' at the news of the assassination, while Swinburne, once more the vengeful sprite who had capered in his rooms at Oxford before a portrait of Napoleon III's attempted assassin, Felice Orsini, added a cheery postscript to his letter to Rossetti:

'Seriously, I cannot but feel that to all of us—us others—the news of a successful tyrannicide must and should be as . . . the news of a king's recovery from sickness to royalists.'

And in 'Russia: An Ode', published in 1890 in spite of Watts' hesitations, Swinburne sternly urged the subjects of Czar Alexander III to do their sacred duty too. The terrors and miseries of Russia could only have one violent end. 'Smite!' Swinburne thunders from the peaceful heights of Putney.

Smite, and send him howling down his father's way!

This was the old, the true Swinburne, a phoenix rising at last out of the dusty immolation of The Pines.

Night hath none but one red star—Tyrannicide!

The young kindled to it at once. 'No poem of my time thrilled me more', wrote the poet William (later Sir William) Watson to Watts-Dunton years later, when Swinburne was dead, 'and it showed the man in his noblest light, as a great and fiery hater of oppression—the light in which I shall choose to think of him to the last'. To the last, Swinburne was an unbudging enemy of Imperial Russia, and of any country which made a gesture of friendship towards her. Heaven did not listen this time to his instructions on liquidating Alexander III. He looked at the son, Nicholas II, with an equally baleful eye. When the new Czar, for whom the gods had terrible plans of their own, was about to pay a state call on Paris in September 1896, he wrote to Watts from his usual autumn visit to his mother, childishly disappointed that the weather had not turned up trumps and ruined the diplomatic accord. 'Don't you wish that yesterday's hurricane could have fallen on Paris during the coming visit of the Czar? I do.' He was outraged by 'the fawning, servile, prostitute hospitality of the strumpet Republic to "that excellent grand tyrant of the earth" '. It reminded him of a 'tremendous passage in Ezekiel' about the whore who gave gifts to all her lovers to bribe them to come to her. He was a great and admiring reader of the 'Divine Author'. 'Revoltingly obscene and perhaps incomparably bloodthirsty' though he was, Swinburne could not help admitting that from the literary point of view he was sometimes 'a god of genius'—almost comparable to His servant Dante. Swinburne's letters abounded in Scripture quotations, in a way that would have surprised the clerics who had thundered their disapproval of 'Poems and Ballads'.

He had never felt the same towards France since the Franco-Russian entente ten years earlier. It was as strange and painful as feeling anger towards one of his own family. If in his youth he had liked to regard himself as an adopted Italian by right of the heart, he had once spoken quite seriously to Watts of 'my loyalty as a Frenchman'. There was, of course, his highly debatable, pleasantly romantic strain of Polignac blood. On that far-off walking tour in Auvergne with Richard Burton they had visited the high, ghostly ruins of the Château de Polignac, and Swinburne, dancing by Burton's side, had done the honours of the place with the grace of a young seigneur showing a friend round the old family home. But his whole background and upbringing had been rooted firmly in 'France, the wellbeloved'. His Swinburne ancestors, in exile for their Stuart loyalties, had taken refuge there more than once, and had liked it so well that they lingered on after the need was past. They had particular ties with Bordeaux. An earlier Thomas Swynbourne, awarded land in France by Richard II after making a crusade to the Holy Land, is recorded as having become mayor of the town in 1404. Swinburne's grandfather, Sir John, was born near Bordeaux and educated in France. French was the second language in which Swinburne sported as early and naturally as he embraced the sea. His filial devotion to Victor Hugo strengthened his feeling of being almost a Frenchman.

And yet after the well-beloved moved towards Russia, he never really forgave her. The Third Republic, which he had hailed with such ecstatic rapture, had long ago disappointed him. As with Italy, his fervour and his songs cooled directly the cause was won. Hugo was now dead. When the French press dared to criticize England, Swinburne directed some sharp fire across the Channel, and the Paris journals rattled a hail of hostile comment back against the dignified front door of The Pines. The three most violent sonnets, 'The Russ and the Frenchman', and another bitter poem 'Russo-Gallia', written at white heat in 1886 at the time of the appalling show of amiabilities between the well-beloved and the worst-hated, were gingerly gathered up by Watts and dropped into a drawer out of sight before they could ignite anything or anybody. Swinburne must have given in reluctantly, as he agreed to Watts' ruling on the quashing of another particularly uninhibited sonnet on the Home Rule question, referring to the 'reptile rage of Ireland' foaming and cowering at the heel of 'the lion England'. (After he had gone, however, we note old Watts-Dunton digging out the manuscripts of the Russo-French poems and, perhaps reflecting that nothing could hurt Algernon now, selling them to the acquisitive and helpful Mr. Thomas J. Wise.)

Dark suspicions of what France was up to continued to trouble Swinburne. When young William Rothenstein succeeded in being asked to The Pines one August day in 1895 to draw the Bard, fidgeting wretchedly in the torture of a new suit—the unease is visible in the nervy, delicate drawing which later went to the Municipal Gallery of Modern Art, Dublin—he expounded to Rothenstein the tetchy theory that the French were 'always ready to fly at our throats, and would crush us at any moment' if given the chance. He and Watts also kept a sharp, distrustful eye on the increasing militarism of Germany. The one good thing he had ever thought of the Germans, he had written long ago to 'poor dear George' Powell, the lover of Wagner, was that they 'did' music 'so much better than any other people that no one even comes second'. Now Swinburne reduced his fears into unspeakably bad verse that caused many more than Edmund Gosse to bewail the dulling of Apollo's bright bow after years of collecting dust in Putney.

> Let the German touch hands with the Gaul
> And the fortress of England must fall. . .
> Our time once more is over,
> Once more our end is near;
> A bull without a drover
> The Briton reels to rear,
> And the van of the nations is held by his betters,
> And the seas of the world shall be loosed from his
>     fetters. . .

Did Watts praise, in his usual nourishing way, such pathetic fallings-off from the wonderful days? Undoubtedly he did. He fired off some booming patriotic salvoes of verse himself from time to time, which were greatly admired among his friends. He believed firmly in the divine right of England as the superior nation elected above all the other, unhappily for themselves, foreign nations. Cecil Rhodes was one of his heroes; he wrote a laborious sonnet-sequence to him. The romantic heart which made Watts cherish those oddly inappropriate dreams about gypsy girls and the open road was fired by the thought of Africa. The mind which was constantly brooding over gigantic schemes for impossible novels about picturesque men of action, and ancient castles and curses, and wild Balkan fastnesses as remote from the comfortable shabbiness of the Putney villa as the cold land-

scapes of the moon, of course thrilled to the adventure of
'1,500,000 square miles in a glorious climate', now coloured
a satisfactory red on the map. Masses of his fellow countrymen were in the same euphoric mood. An aggressive imperi-
alism echoes through the popular newspapers and the
music-hall ditties of the day, often belted out by uniformed
ladies who tapped their abundant thighs dashingly with
military canes as they sang. There seemed to be a note of
desperation under all the noise, perhaps. The insistence on
England's greatness, richness, invincibility, sprang from
Englishmen's uneasy suspicion that, as Swinburne dolefully
chanted, threats to all three were lurking somewhere ahead
in the new century that would shortly begin. It was
impossible that Swinburne should fail to catch the fever, as
he had been swept into the emotion of the Golden Jubilee.
He was always like a piece of sensitive paper which could
take an impression and reproduce anything it chose with
wonderful fidelity.

Swinburne's attacks in the eighties on the fighters for
Home Rule for Ireland and, at the end of the century, on the
Boers were applauded at The Pines and by the patriotic ladies
of his family, but liberal opinion was outraged. It was a grie-
vous shock to find the poet of liberty, Mazzini's and Hugo's
poet, pouring out violent abuse of Ireland, for daring to
demand that she should cut away from Queen Victoria and
govern herself, and later, castigating the two small republics
of belligerent Dutch farmers who were giving England (to
world applause) such humiliating military setbacks in the
Transvaal. Swinburne saw not the slightest awkwardness
or any change of principle in this attitude. He defended
himself irascibly from the criticisms of friends and of his
disappointed public. Did the fools point out that Italy's
struggle to free herself from Austrian rule in the forties had
many points of resemblance to the bitter Irish battle for

137

independence? Mazzini, he averred with confidence—not entirely shared by all his critics, however—would certainly have been utterly opposed to the breaking off of the legislative union between England and Ireland. And then some anonymous scribblers of the Gladstone faction (Gladstone, Swinburne's abhorrence, split the Liberal Party in 1886 when he was converted to the policy of Home Rule for Ireland) sneered at him as a defector. Just twenty-five years ago, they reminded their readers, young Mr. Swinburne, now singing a different middle-aged tune over the appalling stabbing to death of the Viceroy, Lord Frederick Cavendish, and his Under-Secretary, Charles Burke, in Phoenix Park, Dublin, had appealed passionately against the death sentence passed on three Fenians for murdering a policeman in Manchester. Swinburne dashed off an elaborately scornful letter to *The Times* refuting the ridiculous charge of apostasy brought against him by these 'nameless persons', which had caused him 'considerable amusement', he said. He ex-explained the fine points of the morality of homocide. The Irishmen who killed the unfortunate policeman in Manchester had been attempting to rescue a friend he had arrested. There had been considerable, though unsuccessful, public agitation at the time for a reprieve of the 'Manchester Martyrs'. How could an unpremeditated killing be compared with the cold-blooded, cowardly crime in Dublin? Swinburne could appreciate the distinction perfectly, even if others could not. Dashing impetuously to a friend's rescue would have appealed to him in his youth. He had no fear of anything, except lifts. There was the time when he was waylaid in a lonely part of Putney Heath by a half-crazed, strongly built individual who had some grudge against him and threatened him with a stick. Swinburne had ignored man and stick and walked serenely on, reducing the attempt to the ridiculous. When Watts, horrified, spoke of taking out a warrant against his aggressor, he had laughed at the idea. No, open danger was one thing, but a treacherous knifing in the back was another.

Many more letters to the newspapers winged their way angrily out of Putney, and some brickbats were hurled back over the stone pineapples. *Punch* parodied his 'The Commonweal: A Song for Unionists' (in which he attacked Gladstone and Charles Stewart Parnell and the pledge of Home Rule for Ireland) in a cartoon showing Swinburne, all hair and temper, reeling out 'The Common Squeal; A Song for Shriekers', with a few sample shrieks appended. His friends were not always sympathetic by any means. When his dear, revered Mrs. Lynn Linton, Landor's 'daughter' of the old poet's last years, was so unwise as to put her name in print to some cordial sentiments about the Irish leader, William O'Brien, he hauled her over the coals severely. He was thunderstruck, he said, that she had shown admiration for such a 'dastardly and indecent miscreant'. Landor, their mutual god, could only have shown hatred and abhorrence of the bloody, cowardly terrorist acts of the whole Hibernian gang, as did 'Your affectionate friend, A. C. Swinburne'. Mrs. Lynn Linton, it appears, hastily saw the errors of her ways, but other misguided spirits did not.

And when feeling over the Boer War, which broke out in 1899, divided the country into pro-war hawks and pro-Boer doves, and Swinburne declared himself with the first group, many of his old circle could not keep him company—including, to his sorrow, another old and forever to be thanked friend, the exiled German political writer, Karl Blind, the leader of the Baden insurrection in the forties, who had introduced him to Mazzini in 1867. Some individuals, indeed, were still crass enough to take for granted the side on which Mr. Swinburne's illustrious muse would naturally be singing. A journalist named Clayden wrote to The Pines in August, 1899, enclosing a report of a public meeting which had been called a month earlier 'to Protest against Reckless Threats of War with the Transvaal'. 'Believing that you will sympathize with our efforts and be willing to co-operate in our endeavour to spread a knowledge of the true facts of the case, we ask you to allow us to add your name to our Committee.' Thus wrote the surely reckless Mr. Clayden, and received back a short, sharp broadside: 'Dear Sir: I am about the last man in England who would allow his name to be added to your Committee.'

Ten years later, when Swinburne died, Bernard Shaw added some musing and not unfriendly comments to all that was being written about him. 'An odd phenomenon', Shaw ruminated, 'this supporter of Dublin Castle who was a republican and regicide when Russia was in question; always . . . great on paper, insignificant on Putney Hill.' What a pity it was that Swinburne had not done more work as a translator. 'Putney could not set him thinking, but the Periclean age could . . . He was a splendid sounding board vibrating grandly to other people's conceptions, and if he had spent his life in turning Greek thought into English music he would have enriched the nation enormously.'

The nation never enriched Swinburne with any honour, as it turned out, and he steadfastly declined any distinctions from other quarters, such as an honorary degree from Oxford. Watts' fond dream that dear Algernon would one day take his rightful place and come into his own never became daylight fact. In 1892, Tennyson died and was buried in Westminster Abbey. Swinburne did not go to the ceremony, although his last exchange with the Laureate had been affectionate. He had written, with encouragement from Watts, an ode to Tennyson on his eighty second birthday in 1891, and the Laureate had thanked him with emotion. '. . . In your Birthday Song I find metre and diction as lovely as ever; but the touch of kindliness towards myself . . . moves the heart of the old Poet more, I think, than even the melody of your verse.' Yet Swinburne was not among his mourners in the Abbey, for the same reason that he had stayed away from Robert Browning's funeral three years before. He detested all functions, but a funereal one was the worst. His antagonism to the rites of Christian burial was as vehement as his horror at the idea of taking a newborn infant, a divine angel from heaven, to the font and proclaiming it 'a child of wrath'. He and Watts often discussed it. Watts knew exactly how he felt. It had been agreed solemnly between them that if Walter, the elder by five years, should turn out to be the survivor, he would see to it that Algernon would be laid simply in the earth without any priest assisting in the proceedings.

So the old Poet was now dead, and who would succeed him? Many people's thoughts travelled to Putney and the celebrated retreat. Queen Victoria herself appears for one brief and charming moment, a stout little black widow figure inclining her head in majestic salute to The Pines, the future Widow of Putney Hill who would outlive her own two Alberts, outlive Victoria's son and grandson and great-grandson, and sit on in a changed world, respectably buttoned up with her memories behind the blue memorial cameo pinned to her bosom by the old London County Council. Clear and small comes the good Queen's voice, speaking a stately line to her Prime Minister, perhaps, when he attended Her Majesty to consider Tennyson's successor. 'I am told that Mr. Swinburne is the best poet in my dominions', she is reported to have intoned before vanishing abruptly. Did the immortal royal observation reach Watts' sharp ears and rejoice them? But it was not enough. Though many of her subjects agreed with it, too many impossibilities stood in the way of the preposterous notion of Swinburne being invited to step into Tennyson's shoes. Was it thought of the early 'imprudences', or his often stated attitude to the Established Church, or (this was said to be the official reason, so Watts' fears at the time seem to have been well-founded) that he had offended by 'something he once wrote about the Czar'? Anyway, no frog footman with an immense blazoned envelope pushed open the gate between the stone pine-apples. The unexceptionable poet Alfred Austin was appointed Laureate.

Poor Watts may have been bitterly disappointed, but we can be contentedly sure that Swinburne was not. Unless Walter had managed to work a miracle of persuasion, he would certainly have refused the post. He did not take it with proper gravity. Just before Tennyson's death, he had quoted to Watts some loyal lines composed by one Reverend Laurence Eusden, a clergyman who had been George II's dutiful Laureate and was now deservedly silted up in the dust and rubbish of the past.

> Hail, mighty Monarch! [Eusden had piped] whose desert alone
> Would without birthright raise thee to a throne;
> Thy virtues shine pe-cu-li-ar-ly nice,
> Ungloom'd with a confinity to vice.

Perhaps, Swinburne suggested slyly, Walter would show this as a worthy model to the Laureate next time he ran down for a night to the Tennysons at Aldworth, where all the bedroom doors were inscribed with the names of knights and ladies in 'Idylls of the King'. Swinburne used to refer to the work as 'Idylls of the Prince Consort'. *Dors en paix, ô mon père! Tu m'avais donné la vie—je te donne la vengeance!* No, he would not have done at all. And when Tennyson died and he was asked to say who he thought should be the new Court Singer, he indifferently mentioned two names—Austin's was not one of them, and neither was one of the younger generation of poets, for he seems to have had curiously little interest in what others were writing. Then he went back into his library, immediately entered the bright, pure world of art which was increasingly the only reality, far from the remote happenings he hymned so mechanically from time to time, and forgot all about it.

# IX

SWINBURNE CONTINUED the practise of going off, generally once and sometimes twice a year, for leisurely visits to his family in the country. The details of the journey were still worked out carefully in advance by Watts and Lady Jane, as though planning the shipment of some immensely precious object that might easily go astray on the railway and end up in a dreadful condition miles from its destination. They never precisely voiced their fears of how perdition was likely to pounce on Algernon sitting happily reading in the slow from Paddington, but they continued to confer uneasily before each expedition. If Mr. Watts could not accompany him, we find Lady Jane writing in 1892, perhaps 'as it is a short journey, only a hour and a half from London to Bentley, our station, you might think that Algernon might do it alone'. He was then fifty-five, and Watts seems to have written back soothingly that he could probably manage it without mishap. But the London station to which the little package was taken and consigned on its perilous course was not always Paddington, as in the days when the Swinburne ladies lived at Bradford-on-Avon. Lady Jane had moved from Leigh House in 1887, to Swinburne's regret. He had grown fond of the place and of the lonely rolling Wiltshire countryside, over which he tirelessly walked for hours in all weathers. It was the first bit of England, apart from the Putney commons, round which he had felt a tendril of affection beginning to twine since he had been uprooted twenty-three years ago from the Eden of East Dene and the wild knotted trees of the Landslip and the sea birds screaming on the shore. After they left Leigh House, Lady Jane and the Misses Swinburne seem to have divided their time between London, where Algernon and Mr. Watts often came to luncheon at the house they took in Ennismore Gardens, and a succession of furnished country houses which they rented, sometimes for the summer months, sometimes for a year or two, in various parts of England. Perhaps they were sampling different air and views and neighbours before they settled on a permanent home, of which there was talk now and then, but talk it remained. The restless packing up and flitting off to yet another rambling Rectory or sleepy old Hall in Surrey, in Hampshire, in Warwickshire, continued from year to year, and doubtless the new plan suited everybody. Algernon was not so far away from them in Ennismore Gardens, and his sisters must have enjoyed their spells of emancipation from instructing the little ones at the lodge in the mysteries of pot-hooks and multiplication tables.

Swinburne's devotion to them all seemed to deepen every year. The peaceful High Church atmosphere of his home, quickly oppressive to him in the old days when he had been forced to crawl back and recuperate from the drinking and the rites of the chastising goddesses, folded him on these country visits into 'a delightful groove of quiet family life', as he wrote to Watts. He would have been perfectly happy to stay there, he felt, if it were not for missing Walter every day, and Bertie, and Bertie's mother, Mrs. Mason, of whom he had a high opinion. He worked and walked and amused himself digging about in the libraries of his mother's temporary homes. In the evenings, Mimmie, with Ally, Wibbie, and Abba grouped round her, made an admiring audience while Algernon read his latest poem. The carriage wheels of the local gentry never disturbed the peace, for they knew that his deafness made him shy of new acquaintances. They invited nobody except relations or close friends while he was staying with them. The summer or autumn weeks he passed in the various large, comfortable rented houses were a great change from the cramped villa on Putney Hill, where perpetual smells of cooking, rising from the dark domains below, hung about in the dark little hall. A larger, more cultured, patrician air seems to blow through these pleasant rooms and pleasure-grounds and trim avenues. From Swinburne's descriptions, the scenes in his calm domestic circle have the charm of a Victorian water-colour or a Morris wallpaper. One summer, enormous sunflowers with strange spongy centres of bluish-green or palest saffron looked over the sun-warmed brick walls at him where he sat reading Sir Philip Sidney's 'Arcadia', the fantasy written to please a sister. The ancient book, the ancient little manor, and the sunflowers came together in his mind and made a poem, 'Astrophel'. The slow rural hours of these visits seem to be marked by the grave voice of a church clock chiming across deliciously smelling hay fields. It took him back across the years to his own childhood when he saw the village children tumbling about in the ricks. Then twilight fell, when he and his sisters came home from some outing, and the lamps were lit indoors, and there was the agreeable harmony, to which his ears were attuned through long familiarity, of the four clear Swinburne voices. Everything was so blessedly familiar that his thoughts returned increasingly to the obsessive theme of East Dene and Capheaton and his youth, the lost Arcadia. The furnished houses were probably made personal by various objects he would have known from his earliest days—the cherished portfolio of Turner sketches that always travelled with Lady Jane, for instance, and family silver and china. The

146

butler, Woods, had been with them for many years. And best of all to Swinburne were the intimate little family jokes, the dear old nicknames, the memories and allusions that he could share instantly with his mother and sisters. It was a delightful groove indeed.

From these memories he would presently write the little play, 'The Sisters', in which we find everything—the great house in Northumberland, the cousins who grew up together and fell in love, the floggings at Eton, the rides over the moors and the private theatricals, the old dream of military glory—Reggie Clavering, the hero, has come back wounded from Waterloo, to be agreeably made much of by the girl cousins—and finally, the lovers' preposterous death scene, in the style of his favourite Jacobean tragedies, after swallowing accidentally a poisonous potion which was to be a prop in their theatricals. The critics were cool, but his family liked it.

And yet, in the middle of his happiness at being with them all, he missed Putney. Rambling in the rural solitudes, he looked forward to setting his foot on the suburban grass of 'the Common' again. The Pines was also home. He missed Watts. It was true that when they were apart Watts' solicitous care continued to watch rather touchingly over every detail of Swinburne's welfare as though they were together. He forwarded batches of proofs, and more warm underwear if the weather turned chill, and suddenly needed books. He reported on business interviews with Andrew Chatto; he sent along newspaper cuttings and bulletins of Pines news and London literary gossip, for which he knew Algernon hungered even in contented rustication. If Algernon mentioned in a letter that he felt sluggish and could not keep awake in the strong air of the Swinburne ladies' latest domicile, back by return of post came a box of liver pills. One scorching August, he complained of having flying pains in the head, not surprisingly, after having walked for over four hours in the blazing sun, and immediately came Watts' anxious reply. Could not Miss Alice drive into the nearest town where there was a draper's shop and see if she could buy her brother a puggaree—a sort of muslin scarf which Victorian gentlemen in the tropics wore tied round their hats and falling down behind to keep the sun off their necks? Swinburne thought this very funny. A puggaree, he wrote back, was an article only known to him as having once supplied Gabriel Rossetti, who sometimes made up bawdy limericks to amuse his friends, with an extremely useful rhyme. His sister did not think he could put up with such an article, even if they could run one to earth. (We have to regret that they did not, and that Max Beerbohm did not make a drawing of him later on, streaking along a country lane like a tiny fiery meteor with a long muslin tail.) But he thanked Walter affectionately for his kind thoughtfulness, all the same.

There is some pathos in the earnestness of Watts' ceaseless supervision. He was Swinburne's senior; his health was good, but his eyesight was giving trouble, and he was getting tiresomely deaf himself. Eyes and ears were like advance scouts warning him of the marching years. As he packed up pills and instructions, or, at home at The Pines, insisted on Algernon changing his wet trousers when he came cheerfully racing back to luncheon through a rain storm, did it occur to him to wonder who would look after the poor dear fellow like this if he were suddenly not there? It must have done many times, and not only to him. There was a nasty moment in September, 1895, when Swinburne was luckily staying with his family in Solihull, a then still rural spot near Birmingham, and Watts suddenly went down with a serious and painful illness. Swinburne seemed a little hazy as to its nature, for he wrote plaintively to Walter, in bed in Putney and being nursed by Mrs. Mason, admitting that 'whereabouts "the bladder" is' was as mysterious to him as the existence of a puggaree had been. Such were the delicacies of Victorian behaviour that he did not like to ask any member of this godly feminine household to enlighten him. He does not sound acutely anxious about Watts, but in a letter Lady Jane writes to the now convalescent invalid a few weeks later we are conscious of the faint rustle of a bosom exhaling a profound sigh of relief. She is 'quite thankful' to hear better news of him. He must certainly be 'very prudent' for a long time to come, and what a dreadful worry Mrs. Mason must have had, and how merciful it is that he has a clever doctor. For what could be done about Algernon, she is surely asking herself, if anything happened to Mr. Watts, and The Pines ceased to exist? It was a fearful thought. She was eighty-six and in frail health. Her portrait shows her, a beautiful, aristocratic old lady, swaddled in lace, who has laid down her book and is staring sadly, thoughtfully into space. She was not likely to rival her sister-in-law, Julia Swinburne, Aunt Ju, that breath of racy life from another century, who had died not long ago, only two years short of a hundred; who had remained chirpy to the end; who had stumped off for a long ramble across wet moorland on the arm of her admiring nephew Algernon when she was a mere ninety-two; and had talked, and doubtless eaten, more on that same visit than anyone else in the exhausted family party. No, Lady Jane was not an Aunt Ju. Soon there would only be Ally, Wibbie, and Abba left. They were practical, bright-tempered women. They adored Algernon, they were tremendously proud of him; it was doubtful if they wanted to live with him. Probably he felt the same. The distance between Ennismore Gardens, Knightsbridge, and Putney Hill was just the right distance to have between them. So Lady Jane must have heard with inexpressible thankfulness that Mr. Watts had such an excellent doctor.

As it turned out, The Pines remained solid as a rock, and what split up and disappeared was the whole of Swinburne's deeply loved family background. In a little over a decade, all but one of its members were gone. The youngest sister, Abba—Isabel Swinburne—was the only survivor, and she would outlive both Swinburne and Watts and see the beginning of the first World War. Edward, the young brother, had already broken up the circle. Indeed he seems always to have stood outside it. There is something mysterious about Edward, whom we last saw dryly advising Watts that it would be wise to make it difficult for Algernon to get hold of the two thousand pounds their mother had made over to him, in case he should wish to throw too much of it away 'on some book'. The scorn is evident; he cared only for music. After his marriage to his Berlin cousin, Olga Thumann, they seem to have lived abroad. Now and then he turns up to stay with his mother for a while, but a cloud descends, there is illness and domestic trouble, and suddenly in July, 1891, Edward is dying alone among strangers in a house in St. John's Wood—a part of London that had once had such bizarre associations for Swinburne. There is a hint of seediness, of dark experiences never referred to, for the family knew nothing of his return to England. The people of the house had looked after him kindly, but they had not written to the Swinburnes until it was too late.

The news came when Swinburne was on one of his visits —this time to Brockhampton Park, in Herefordshire. It was already an anxious time for them all. Lady Jane had been dangerously ill, and was only just beginning to recover. The letters that went from Brockhampton Park to The Pines make us regret that Swinburne never wrote another novel after 'Lesbia Brandon' and 'Love's Cross-Currents', for his description of the worried household is like a good chapter out of a Victorian three-decker. We see it all—his sisters bustling in and out of the sick-room to take their turns watching their mother with the 'cheery stoicism' (he borrows the phrase from Carlyle) shown by women of their upbringing in moments of crisis, whereas the dear old housekeeper, who used to be the Swinburne children's nurse, feels it only decent to go round looking as though she were on her way to the gallows. And to make everything doubly, trebly worse, there are guests in the house—French guests, who were there when Lady Jane was taken ill, who do not immediately make excuses and go home, who stay on, vivaciously expectant of entertainment, while Swinburne gallantly tries to 'do the civil'. It must have been a strain, but the duration of a Victorian visit appears to be sacred. At last they go, thank heavens, and Swinburne expresses his relief by walking twenty miles or so at top speed in pouring rain. We can imagine Watts frowning as he got to that bit. Had he remembered to change his socks as soon as he got back to Brockhampton Park? Very probably not.

Then, just as the household was relaxing with the assurance that Mimmie was over the worst, the awful news about Edward arrived. Woods, the trusted butler, was sent off to St. John's Wood to look after him, and Alice, declining Algernon's offer to escort her, followed with her maid. She was not in time. Edward's heart had failed, He was only forty-three. Woods began immediately, as though the lonely death-bed had been a dishevelled drawing-room distressing to his sense of what was seemly for the family, tidying everything neatly away and restoring the occasion to its proper dignity. He supervised the removal of the body to Lady Jane's house in Ennismore Gardens and arranged for the funeral at Bonchurch, where Admiral Swinburne and

Edith were buried. Mr. Longbourne, the family solicitor, arrived to support him. Edward's wife was absent, and 'we do not even know where the woman is now', Swinburne wrote contemptuously to Watts, adding a fierce 'Thank heaven!' His letters giving the news were emotional. Though he and Edward had never been close, the death plunged him in sorrowful thoughts of the past. It sent him away from this house full of plump, red-eyed, middle-aged women, back to East Dene and the happy days, but also, like a child in the dark calling down to the reassuring adult world of safe lamplight, home to The Pines.

His letters breathe a desolate longing to have Watts there, in the solid, comforting flesh. 'Please send me a line as soon as you get this.' The sight of a written word, he says, would be almost as good as the sight of Walter's face or the clasp of his hand. 'I hardly know why I write this to-night, unless . . . because my heart and mind instinctively turn to you first of all in any time of trouble.' Watts, so much weaker than he intellectually (though he loyally never admits this; Walter is 'the greatest and most scholarly critic of English literature now living'; Walter's sonnets are read to the receptive home circle along with his own, and the ladies' admiration gushes back to The Pines), but so much stronger as a man, is the rock without which he would founder. The pathetic death in St. John's Wood, with only Woods turning up at the last moment to supply a face and a voice from home, might have been his own end in Guildford Street thirteen years ago, watched over by faithful Mrs. Magill. 'I cannot but keep thinking,' he muses, '. . . how long since —how many years ago—I should have died as my poor dear brother has just died, if instead of the worst of wives I had not found the best of friends; and how strong and healthy and happy the poor fellow whom I remember in my school holidays as the brightest of baby boys might have been at

Bertie Mason

*Photo reproduced by courtesy of Mr and Mrs Eric Mason*

Clara Watts-Dunton, at about the time of her marriage in 1905

this hour if instead of the best of friends he had not found the worst of wives.'

Meanwhile, there is no time to send 'my mourning' to Bonchurch, as Walter suggests, so will he bring it with him when he joins the family party there? Watts was to be the only mourner who was not a Swinburne. 'Please also bring my *tall hat* (it is in a hat-box under my bed)'. It was the age of funeral emporiums, of grief measured in depth of crape, of black borders to writing-paper, and black sealing-wax dropping jetty tears on envelopes, and black ribbons threaded in even little girls' petticoats. When Queen Victoria died ten years later, a sort of freak black blizzard engulfed the nation overnight. It is comic to find Swinburne, who detested and avoided funereal occasions, fussing over his mourning, but there was always that ingrained streak of sticking to the formalities of behaviour. His mother could not go to the funeral. She would be at Brockhampton Park, lying thinking mournfully of them all, with his sister Wibbie—Charlotte, who seemed to be the delicate one— left behind to keep her company. Algernon must represent her, fittingly equipped to stand in the churchyard at Bonchurch and listen quietly to the words of a Christian rite that he utterly and passionately disbelieved. So we find him anxiously cautioning Watts not to buy him a new tall hat—the one under the bed was perhaps past its first gloss of youth—in case there is any mistake over size. His head was so immense that once in his boyhood, when his hat was blown into the Channel as he was crossing from France, it was very difficult to find a sufficiently roomy replacement.

Swinburne's world was about to shrink permanently to the scale of The Pines. Soon he would not leave it again on any more visits to the ample, well-run country houses that reminded him of his youth. Lady Jane was the gentle but surprisingly strong centre of the family circle. When she

153

died in 1896, the pattern changed completely. The Misses Swinburne did not keep up the custom of renting large places for the summer months. The charming old-fashioned household of women, in which the elder son had settled back every year with a nod of affectionate recognition to a dazzling boy called Algernon Swinburne, came to an end. The tall hat left its box under the bed for more sad journeys to Bonchurch. Wibbie followed their mother three years later, and Ally died in 1903. Of the five children who had shouted and climbed the ilex trees and ridden their ponies along the cliff tracks at East Dene, only Algernon and Isabel were left.

*　　*　　*

*Being mortals, we have suffered.* So Swinburne had written philosophically when poor dear George Powell disappeared, taking with him a whole corner of the old life. It was no good wailing. But after the dissolving of the tightly attached family knot, everything seems to fall apart a little bit at the centre of things, to become diffuse and floating and a trifle indistinct. Walter was the solid comfort to which he clung more than ever now, and the world of books was increasingly the only real one. He was busy preparing his last book of poems, 'A Channel Passage', which includes the beautiful, melancholy vision called 'The Lake of Gaube', and he was wading irritably through the proofs of the first four fat volumes of the 'Collected Works'—they eventually totalled eleven, poems and plays—which Mr. Chatto published in 1904. He had taken great pains over the long 'Dedicatory Epistle' that prefaced the edition, addressed to 'my best and dearest friend', Walter Theodore Watts-Dunton—for somewhere or other in the nebulous and rather unimportant world outside The Pines, Watts had decided to cease being Watts and had adopted his mother's maiden name, hyphenated to his own. Swinburne had dedicated other poems besides 'Tristram of Lyonesse' to his friend in the years since they set up house together, but this tribute has to emphasize the gratitude and affection even more strongly. It was to be fixed, for posterity to see, to the final statement of his creative life, his last will and testament— for that is what he clearly intends the essay to be—of what he believed and had tried to do in poetry. Walter—who else?—was named as sole legatee. Without him, the edition would have been several volumes shorter, which some people, to be sure, persist in thinking ungratefully would have been better for Swinburne's eventual place among the immortal sons of Apollo. 'Infinitely better', observes Sir Edmund Gosse, his spectacles flashing formidably. And what happened when Gosse and his curiously gifted colleague, Thomas J. Wise, edited the big Bonchurch edition of Swinburne—twenty volumes this time—in 1926? He cut out the 'Dedicatory Epistle' entirely. Watts-Dunton had been dead for twelve years, but it is never too late to pay off old scores. At one time, Gosse told Wise, he had known Swinburne, through and through, better than anyone. And then the insufferable provincial solicitor had carried Swinburne off to Putney. And then Swinburne had changed, had blown cool, had started to talk, like a brilliant ventriloquist, in someone else's voice. Even in retrospect, Gosse plainly could not bear the thought. The 'best and dearest friend' was struck unforgivingly, unforgivably, off the record.

About this time, three young men were invited to journey to Putney and meet the great legend, and they have all described their visits for us. One caller was, of course, Max Beerbohm. Another was a young Eton master, Arthur Christopher Benson, a son of the Archbishop of Canterbury, who went to have luncheon at The Pines in 1902. He had made himself agreeable to Watts-Dunton because he was planning to write a monograph on Gabriel Rossetti, and after luncheon they were going to talk about the other celebrated friendship. As he ate (soup, chicken, plovers' eggs—The Pines keeps a better table, it seems, than Beerbohm's memories of the perennial roast mutton and apple tart), Benson turned upon old Watts-Dunton a cool, shrewd eye. Considering that he was a friend of Edmund Gosse, what he afterwards wrote in his journal was, on the whole, not unfair, and much of it was funny and pathetic. He noted the solid bourgeois furnishings of the shabby but comfortable house, the smells of food in the hall and fragrant leather bindings in Swinburne's room, the odd, shabby attire of the two little hosts, and their obvious devotion to each other. It was 'pleasant to see', he says, 'how they paid each other such fine compliments, and showed such distinguished consideration'. He left to go back to Eton, feeling 'much touched' by their kindness to him. Swinburne had obviously taken to him greatly. 'You must come again!' he had said, shaking hands warmly, 'I suppose you were at Eton about my time?' 'My dear fellow', said Watts-Dunton, 'Mr. Benson's a *young* man!' 'Of course, of course!' said the Bard—but we can imagine how vaguely, for everybody was beginning to look roughly the same age, time had turned the wrong end of the telescope, and he, who could easily see back to people and places still wonderfully bright and large after forty or fifty years, sometimes had difficulty in keeping track of the tiresome pygmy days and weeks. Benson carried away with him the memory of one who looked unexpectedly like 'a little, rather faded don'—most of the visitors to The Pines at that period were similarly surprised, and relieved, not to encounter the excitable little red-haired apparition of so many stories, leaping about the room and screaming like a cockatoo. What he principally remembered with respect was 'a sense of the real genius of Swinburne's mind, the air of intellectual fervour in which he seemed to live habitually and without effort, and his complete abstraction from all ordinary considerations. He was like a man living in a dream of art, and without any ripple or murmur of the world penetrating his solitary paradise'.

The third youthful caller was Alfred Noyes, the poet, who talked about it on a B.B.C. programme in 1957, when he was an old man himself. The household had aged a few more years since Mr. Benson had observed it. Swinburne was seventy, young Noyes had written a poem in his honour that was published in the *Fortnightly Review*, and an invitation to dinner at The Pines was the result. The guest was so excited that he was not at all sure what he ate, though he had a notion that some sort of spectral roast lamb and a whisper of mint sauce floated past. The name of Swinburne was still a marvellously thrilling one to the young. Only a few years back when he was at Oxford, Noyes had an undergraduate friend who always took off his hat when he passed the gate of the famous house on Putney Hill and solemnly chanted: 'I believe in Chaucer, Shakespeare, Shelley, Keats, and Swinburne'. It was no wonder that now, seated at the dinner table listening to the two deaf old men (Watts-Dunton was almost stone-deaf, too, by this time) exchanging 'extremely interesting shouts', he felt that he was in a sort of dream. He felt so safe, indeed, in the cross-fire of shouts and his modest role as a young, awe-struck listener that he risked a mundane remark about the weather, which of course would not get over any better than some earlier, more intelligent observations had fared. But horrors! Swinburne noticed the guest's moving lips, and promptly shouted to Watts-Dunton to know what he had said. The poor young man was struck so dumb by this that his hosts concluded he must be deaf, too, and re-doubled their efforts. After a good deal of frantic bellowing all round,

Noyes roared a hastily improvised question about the influence of Keats on Matthew Arnold, and Swinburne happily agreed. He had been 'a little suphurous' at the start of the evening, Noyes recalled, until the young man had reached over and opened the bottle of beer with which his little hands had been futilely fumbling. Then he became exquisitely gracious. And how he talked, pouring out in a torrent of marvellous images a description of a walk along the rocky shore of the North Sea! The walk had taken place very many years ago, but it was as clear to him in every detail as his exercise on Putney Heath that morning, and perhaps clearer.

To Swinburne, we feel, these visitors—and many more who have given us accounts, delightful or malicious, of pilgrimages to Putney—were only shadows passing and leaving scarcely a trace on the still air of his 'solitary paradise'. It was very different when one of the few surviving old friends came to see him, or when Isabel's short, stout figure descended at The Pines. Those were gala days. And then his cousin Mary, the now widowed Mrs. Disney Leith, had suddenly bustled out of her long silence in Scotland and seemed as warm and lively as though they had not been parted for a day. He was delighted to have her back. Up she sprang, the old Mary, spirited as ever, asking him if he remembered this and that from their youth, sending him primroses, rattling away for his amusement in a not very secret code which they had invented for letters when he was at Eton. They gossiped about her grandchildren and her annual trips to Iceland, with which country she was conducting a late but passionate love affair, and exchanged news of how their work at the moment was going—Mrs. Leith wrote novels and poems. Swinburne ploughed loyally, though hazily, through the manuscript she sent him—in 'your beautiful handwriting', so much easier on the eye than

158

the soulless production of a typewriter, a piece of machinery he mistrusted as thoroughly as he did a lift—of her translation of a modern Icelandic play. It was rather difficult to remember who was who in it, he criticized mildly. In return, he sent her proofs of his play, 'Rosamund, Queen of the Lombards', and dedicated it to her. She was second only to Isabel on the tiny list of names to whom Mr. Chatto was instructed to despatch all his volumes as soon as they were published.

The list had shrunk as the years went by. William Rossetti was on it, of course, The Collected Edition would be sent to him volume by volume, Swinburne wrote affectionately in 1904, but to hardly anyone else. 'Who is there to send to, for that matter?' he asked William rather pathetically. He was housebound in The Pines, convalescing after a dangerous attack of double pneumonia. 'They' had moved him downstairs to his library to sleep as well as to write—there was a coal fire there, and only a little gas-fire in his bedroom—though he came down to the dining-room for lunch and dinner. The most depressing part of it all was that 'They' would not allow him to go out. It was over three months before he set foot on his adored commons again. And when released at last one February morning, he would bolt off at once for a fast six miles walk to Wimbledon and back (doubtless it included a pause and an enthusiastic welcome at the Rose and Crown), and feel much restored. 'The Swinburnes have a tendency to live', Aunt Ju would have commented approvingly.

When he wrote to William Rossetti, however, he was still feeling weak and melancholy as he looked back at all the gaps and losses, not only in his family, but among the old friends who had vanished, or quarrelled with him, or somehow drifted away from the long, exclusive tête-à-tête at The Pines. Edward Burne-Jones, a particularly cherished

159

friend for more than forty years, had died in 1898, two years after 'dear old Topsy', William Morris. Swinburne found it difficult to take in the idea that Ned would never come to see him again, brimming with good talk and fun. George Meredith, another part of the days with Gabriel in Cheyne Walk, was still vigorously alive—a splendid-looking old man, deaf as a post, too, who sat booming magnificently away to the dazzled visitors who journeyed out to his villa at Box Hill. But though he always sent warm messages to Swinburne through Watts-Dunton, they had never been close. It was an inexpressible comfort, therefore, to have William Rossetti, so staunchly, dependably the same. 'My dear and always kind and true friend', Swinburne called him gratefully. He had remained calmly attached to both Swinburne and Watts-Dunton; sneering remarks about Walter did not go unchallenged if he was in hearing range of them. How astonishing to think that he was Gabriel's brother! His fine features, his beard, his sombre dark eyes and lofty brow remind us of a portrait of some befurred donor kneeling with his wife in the bottom corner of an Italian altar-piece, all angels and transfigured saints. There they are on the edge of the divine radiance, looking on in their stiff, earth-bound solidity. William Rossetti, the most earth-bound of his remarkable family, had been on the edge of radiance all his life and had provided a splendid stability to the composition. But the kneeling position is not right for him. Like Swinburne, he was a free-thinker in a family of devout High Anglican women.

Yet, while still an irritable invalid mewed up in the winter gloom of The Pines, Swinburne felt impelled to write to this faithful friend one of his most savage outbursts which, free-thinker though William was, could hardly fail to hurt him. It was a strange, jeering, brutal attack on the religion of his dead sister, Christina Rossetti, the central

160

saint in that other-worldly group he had carried so devotedly on his broad shoulders. William had become her memorialist. Swinburne was writing to thank him for her collected poetical works which he had edited. He had always thought, Swinburne wrote, that 'nothing more glorious in poetry has ever been written' than the verses, 'Passing away, saith the world, passing away'. He had admired Miss Rossetti extravagantly as a poet whose genius, when at her best, was in the direct line of the great English mystics, George Herbert and Henry Vaughan. Her songs of babyhood, he said to Walter, made her 'the spiritual sister of Blake'. And he had felt affection for her, too, as a woman whose quiet strength and goodness roused the peculiar tenderness he kept for the innocent creatures in plush bonnets lying in their baby-carriages on Putney Heath, or for bright spirits such as Lizzie Siddal. William had sent him Christina's table-cover as a memento when she died, and he had thanked William with emotion for a 'really and naturally sacred relic', which he would always treasure. It turned out to be too large for his own table, so he draped it over the sofa where nobody ever reclined, since it was a convenient dumping ground for stacks of books.

The relic was in sight, then, as Swinburne sat writing to William. Christina's poetry, he wrote, was indeed 'rich in beauty', but—here the reverent, admiring note changes, the vituperation pours out in an uncontrollable flood—but 'Good Satan! what a fearful warning against the criminal lunacy of theolatry! It is horrible to think of such a woman—and of so many otherwise noble and beautiful natures'—he is thinking, of course, of Mimmie and the uncomplaining, cheerily dedicated women, his sisters—'spiritually infected and envenomed by the infernal and putrefying virus of the Galilean serpent . . .' He goes on to make a heavy-handed joke about the necessity of sending a mission to what he calls 'the JAH-JAH (pronounced Yah-Yah, "Praise him in his name JAH") Islands' 'to reclaim the degraded inhabitants' who worship a three-headed idol emblematic of '. . . a father and son of the same age and a tertium quid represented as a very old pigeon'. And so on and so on. The curious document, finished the following day, calms down, as though another man had taken over. It ends with a little mild bookish gossip, civil remembrances to a married Rossetti daughter in Italy, and 'kind regards from Watts-Dunton'. William Rossetti seems to have replied with his customary composure, sending along some of Christina's early notebooks which he thought Swinburne would be interested to see.

To the statement of political belief Swinburne wrote to Giuseppe Chiarini in 1872, when he was thirty-five, we can add this fierce re-statement of disbelief, written when he was sixty-seven. Watts-Dunton has left it on record that his antagonism against Christianity increased as he grew older and, at the end, was bitterer than ever. The occasional softer observations about the spiritual beliefs of others, such as Mazzini and Victor Hugo, which he used to drop in letters to Lady Jane, do not appear again. They must have been written to please the loving, anxious special audience. He still hints that he does not rule out the possibility of something, somewhere, after death, but the somewhere does not lead to God.

> I seek not heaven with submission of lips and knees,
> With worship and prayer for a sign till it leap to light. . .

He stated this vigorously in the remarkable poem, 'A Nympholept', written in The Pines years, which he thought was one of his best. The only gods he calls on, he says, are the ones 'hard by, the divine dim powers' who are sensed in the burning mid-day beyond the shade of the forest, the smell of the ferns and moss, and the sound of secret waters running under them. Terror and doubt fade, and he receives the triumphant answer that 'heaven is about me here'. The sky is empty, but unfailingly glorious. In the stout volumes of the 'Collected Works', with their covering address to his best and dearest friend, he has finally packed his baggage for the journey.

# X

SWINBURNE WAS nearing the end of his sixties, and he and Watts-Dunton had been house-mates for over a quarter of a century. The legend had become famous. When people spoke of Swinburne, they saw immediately the villa at the foot of Putney Hill and the old friends seated within, carrying on their unending pedantic duologue, which would only be interrupted when one of them fell abruptly silent.

As it turned out, there was a highly unexpected interruption to the placid flow of life at The Pines. In the spring of 1905, when it occurred, Swinburne was happily busy with the proofs of the long-buried novel which he had written forty years ago. He had agreed to resurrect it. Rereading it was like going back into the past and meeting himself. The hero of the story, Reginald Harewood, was practically a coloured photograph of Algernon Swinburne as a young man, he admitted to William Rossetti, though he hastened to add that 'Redgie's' detestable, harsh, sour father could not have been less like the Admiral. He lingered affectionately over 'Redgie'. As in the verse drama 'The Sisters', the little novel, told in letters, had so much of his youth in it. The complicated families of cousins were there again, and perhaps the complicated passions as well; the aristocratic country-houses, with their huge brick-walled gardens and well-timbered parks and pheasant coverts, that could be heaven for the young; the traumatic beatings at school that had led to the groves of St. John's Wood. The history of 'A Year's Letters' was rather odd. It seems to have appeared inconspicuously in 1877 in a light satirical London magazine just launched under an old name, *The Tatler*. Swinburne had invented a feminine nom-de-plume for himself—perhaps the coloured photograph would have offended his family—but Watts (as he was then) urged him not to publish the novel. He was scandalized by the idea of Algernon appearing, even when disguised in the domino of 'Mrs. Horace Manners', in such a frivolous publication. It was one of the times when the watchdog's disapproving barks were disregarded, however. The magazine was to be edited by an old friend, Thomas Purnell, who had earned Swinburne's undying gratitude for having introduced him to Karl Blind, and thus to Mazzini. Purnell had asked for the youthful manuscript. All Watts' prudent arguments, as he knew ruefully by then, were useless against a chance to repay a debt of the heart.

So now the old story had been dug up out of the dusty files, at Walter's own suggestion. Probably the supply of new subjects at which Swinburne could aim his arrows was running very low. Mrs. Horace Manners, that refined ghostly relict of a diplomat (Swinburne had amused himself at the time by supplying a few biographical details for the lady), vanished into limbo. Chatto published the novel in July that year. Significantly, perhaps, in the light of coming events, Walter had also suggested a new, more romantic title for it: 'Love's Cross-Currents'. To Swinburne's astonishment and pleasure, the brilliant little tragi-comedy was enthusiastically praised by the critics, and sold out the first impression on publication day.

In this pleasantly successful year, something extraordinary happened which seems to set The Pines on its head and to turn our vision of its quiet, devoted inmates topsy-turvy. Various friends of Swinburne and Watts-Dunton ignored the event when writing their account later of the bachelor household. Max Beerbohm makes no mention of it. Sir Edmund Gosse looks stonily the other way. In March, 1905, Watts-Dunton became engaged to a young lady forty-four years his junior. In November that year they were married. He was seventy-three; Miss Clara Reich was twenty-nine. The comfortably frowsy academic establishment presided over so tactfully by Mrs. Mason with assistance from the still more shadowy sister, Miss Theresa Watts, shudders and falls apart. Squawks of indignant disbelief float up the kitchen stairs. The Rossetti ladies quake in their frames, and a quantity of nasty fresh air rushes under the dusty rugs and blows desk papers about as the front door opens and shuts with a purposeful thump, letting in a new arrival. 'No room! No room!' Thus the hosts sitting cosily arguing at that movable feast of a teaparty in Wonderland had chanted when they saw Alice coming, but it was no good. ' "There's *plenty* of room", said Alice indignantly,' and she sat down firmly. The Pines had a new young mistress, or chatelaine, as she later described herself more grandly. The long, virtually tête-à-tête meal was over. The news must have rocked London's literary circles with shock and laughter. Who was she? Few people knew. The *Daily Mirror*, having tried in vain to dig up a photograph of the future Mrs. Watts-Dunton, was obliged to print the nuptial tidings with Mr. Swinburne's well-known features occupying her place beside her betrothed.

Who was Clara Reich, who had the temerity to break into one of the most celebrated, jealously guarded relationships in English letters? We know very little about her, though some years later she wrote an account of her marriage, 'Watts-Dunton and I', and also set down her memories of the everyday routine of 'the Bard' in a work entitled 'The

Home Life of Swinburne'. Watts-Dunton's inflexible taboo against any personal chit-chat about his friend would be ignored, ironically enough, by his widow. Among the masses of trivia through which we stumble after her, trying to imagine how greatly the elderly Pines must have changed now that youth and beauty have come in at the door, there are vague, cloudy patches in which it is difficult to make out exactly how it all came about. There are mysteries. 'My marriage was not one of those unions between May and December which satirists contemplate with malicious enjoyment', she says briskly. Quoting her words in a footnote to the last volume of the great Yale University Press edition of Swinburne's letters, its editor, Mr. Cecil Y. Lang, adds the dry observation: ' "Satirists" to this day purvey the story that Swinburne and Watts-Dunton decided by the toss of a coin which one should marry her'.

Mystery piled on mysteries! For, luckier than the *Daily Mirror*, we can study a photograph of Mrs. Watts-Dunton at the time of her marriage, and the picture of a young woman waiting, like a housemaid come for an interview, in the hall of The Pines while two deaf old gentlemen toss up for her seems to wobble rather badly. She has large, dark eyes under strong brows, a mass of black hair, a round, firm chin, and an enquiring expression. If you added gold hoops and a brilliant scarf, she might have walked out of Watts-Dunton's romantic dreams of the wandering horse-coping Gryengroes, and, indeed, she sat, it seems, for the portrait of Rhona Boswell, the Romany heroine of his 'The Coming of Love', which hung among the Rossetti crayons. It is easier to imagine this determined-looking beauty tossing up to see which *she* would choose, Mr. Swinburne or Mr. Watts-Dunton. Perhaps she really wished to marry The Pines. But the whole thing is something of a shock. We feel as though Esther Summerson has after all united herself to

Mr. Jarndyce, or that she has gone along the shelf into a different volume and wedded both the Cheeryble brothers at once. Whoever married Walter would also be taking on Algernon—that was plain.

And Swinburne, we may feel, must have been much in his friend's thoughts before he decided to marry, or to allow himself, at the end of a resolutely bachelor life, to be married. The latter version seems to have been the one which was more credible to 'satirists' in the world outside The Pines. Yet it made a good deal of sense. A few years ago, Watts-Dunton had been rather seriously ill again. His sisters were getting old, too. Would he not feel easier in his mind about Algernon if there could be someone younger and stronger and gayer about the place—someone, what is more, who already knew the sacred day-to-day time-table of The Pines? His ever-anxious brain must have revolved all these possibilities.

For Clara had been a frequent visitor—this is one of the mysteries over which she skates dreamily in her account of how she came to marry Mr. Jarndyce and be the chatelaine of Bleak House—during the twelve years after she first set foot in it. Did she go to work for Watts-Dunton as one of the secretaries who helped him excavate that mountain of unfruitful labour that was always puzzlingly 'on hand'? She does not say, beyond relating her excitement when he asked her, early in their acquaintance, to make a fair copy for the printer of Swinburne's manuscript of 'The Tale of Balen'. She was a school-girl of sixteen when she was taken along to call at The Pines by her mother, who was a friend of Watts-Dunton. Swinburne was not there, but Watts-Dunton received them very cordially. And presently a pleasant friendship, which might have been supposed to be avuncular on his part and a juvenile crush on hers, seems to have sprung up between him and Mrs. Reich's pretty

A corner in The Pines, showing the painted and carved cabinet

The drawing-room, showing the sofa where Watts-Dunton used to receive visitors, and on which he died. Above the fireplace, "the last and best photograph" of Swinburne

*Photos: Poole, Putney*

The Pines in 1971

*Photo: Ravenna S.*

little daughter. He invited her to a matinée of 'Hedda Gabler'. She called again at The Pines with the offering of a basket of French beans grown in her own garden. An even more generous plan of presenting him with her pet tortoise, a cherished childhood possession, was frustrated when the tortoise churlishly buried himself in the Reichs' flower-beds before he could be translated to the Parnassus heights of Putney. Watts-Dunton went to see Clara act in her school's French play and was enchanted. She seems to have been talented, and would have made the stage her profession if she had not, so oddly, decided to play the part of a chatelaine in Putney instead.

But this jolly version of their relationship is wrong from the start. Mrs. Watts-Dunton, in her candid memoir, corrects it firmly. It was neither avuncular nor girlishly hero-worshipping. It was love. It was a romance as sudden as Swinburne's infatuation with little Bertie Mason. Let us take a look at the lover as another observer saw him about that time. When William Rothenstein went to The Pines to draw Swinburne in 1895—three years after Mrs. Reich, her daughter beside her, rang the doorbell—he regarded the poet's friend with his painter's eye and squeezed out a few tubes of colour in his mind for a quick impression to be dashed down in his journal. 'Old Watts' (the 'Dunton' had not yet been grafted on) was 'a little, round, rosy wrinkled man, with a moustache like a walrus, and a polished dew-lap'. He had evidently been taking an afternoon forty winks; the threadbare house-jacket he had hastily taken off lay on the sofa behind him, and he had donned 'a sort of grey flannel frock-coat' in which to receive the visitor. It is a young man's view, of course. The whiskered Ancient was a vigorous sixty-three at the time, with (his biographers assure us) a singularly unlined brow that gave him a certain youthfulness to the end of his life. And what a different man Miss Reich's expectant dark eyes saw when 'the great critic' greeted her and her mother in the stuffy dining-room of The Pines with so much kindness, showed them the Rossetti drawings, and talked interestingly about the beautiful Mrs. William Morris. Remarkable things had happened instantly when they met. The moment she heard his extraordinarily deep voice pronounce the unremarkable words 'How do you do?', 'a magnetic arrow invisibly thrilled us both . . . and I was profoundly conscious of the fact that I would never be quite the same again'. Polished dewlap, indeed! She saw a mature man of immensely sympathetic charm and warmth, who had made himself indispensable to the greatest lyric poet of the age. He saw—what? An attractive young creature offering, ever so flatteringly and abundantly, the admiration that he had always known was the magic philtre to be administered to genius. He needed it too, in that shrinking and sensitive side of his temperament which was abnormally cast down by any criticism. He was grateful for it. Some such rough conjectures we may make. At any rate, the magnetic arrow was set in action.

It is the last and the greatest surprise which this unexpected and complex man springs on us. So the sensuous mouth noted long ago, before it withdrew behind the immense protective ambush of hair, has declared itself after all. The susceptible heart appears to have given in at the age of seventy-three. It had encountered a formidably determined spirit who would not let it do anything else. The strange girl had clearly made up her mind to marry him. Perhaps she is a spiritual sister to Shaw's Ellie in 'Heartbreak House', who nestled so confidingly and happily on the shoulder of old Captain Shotover. More than forty years later, William Rossetti's daughter, Mrs. Helen Rossetti Angeli, would recall 'this very singular and warm-hearted lady' whom she had got to know as an elderly woman, 'passionately attached to the memory of her husband, and never wearied of speaking of his wonderful care and kindness'. She had no doubts. The owner of the chosen shoulder seems to have had some. Fascinated, helpless, but still attentive to the prudent counsel of Mr. Watts-Dunton, the cool-headed lawyer, he urged her to wait, he pointed carefully to the difference in their ages, he insisted that he could not accept 'the sacrifice you are willing to make for me' without preparing an honest brief for the case against it. Procrastinating as ever, he appears to have taken some time doing so. The waiting went on—we get the impression of some blank pages lightly turned over here—for twelve years. The mysteries of the human heart were never better conveyed. During those years, which included his sudden gratifying success with 'Aylwin' and Swinburne's increasing dependence upon him as one by one the beloved family figures vanished, Watts-Dunton's solid form moved between The Pines and his busy social life, seemingly, one may be sure, quite unchanged. Yet in reality he was leading a tormenting and delightful double existence. He met Clara for brief moments on draughty railway platforms. He called her 'Minaw', the Romany word for 'my own', and had it engraved on a watch for her. If she could not accompany him to a play, she tells us, he telegraphed her between the acts. They saw each other frequently. And at last, in November, 1905, they got married.

Swinburne took the news with the odd, slightly swimming complacency of a man in a dream observing weird events that would startle him very much in waking life. The dream of art, the solitary paradise in which the young Eton master, Arthur Benson, had been touched to feel he now resided permanently, a million light-years away from the feverish desires and quarrels and enthusiasms of the young Swinburne, shut out everything else. Clara Reich, if she impinged at all up to then, was as vaporous as the good Watts ladies had always been. When she first began to come frequently to the house and Swinburne met her in the hall or on the stairs, he would either look through her or, crowding to one side as though he desired to disappear backwards into the wallpaper, give her a doubtful but beautifully courteous bow. The idea that this young person could be anything very special to Walter or was heading towards the leading role of chatelaine of The Pines would not have occurred to him. But they were introduced by Walter at last, and she tells us he was charming. His fine old-fashioned manners were what everybody who met him at The Pines recalled about Swinburne—on days when he was not 'a little sulphurous', that is. Clara must have seemed to him roughly the same age as Bertie had been when his friend used to hammer imperiously on the library door to be admitted. He paid her the highest compliment he could think of by bringing out the treasured 'Black letter book' and watching her eagerly, as she exclaimed over the beasts and fowls with the faces of men and women who stalked and flapped their way through its pages. He bought as a present for her a set of the Sherlock Holmes books—he and Walter were nearly as enthusiastic about Holmes as they were about Charles Lamb. He enjoyed giving little sur-prises; he may even have toyed with the idea of following up with *Aunt Judy's Magazine*. Without comment, no doubt—for, in the dream that life had become, people drifted by, bobbed closer for a second, then were lost to sight with never a trace left floating on the waters—he found that Miss Reich appeared in Cromer when he and Walter took their annual seaside holiday there. The Reich family seem to have had some connection with the resort.

Swinburne's letter to his sister Isabel in which he talks

of Walter's engagement is a curious one. The fact that his dearest and best friend in the world, with whom he has formed a jealously exclusive two-man club for twenty-six years, is now suddenly proposing and seconding a third member, of the wrong sex and inappropriate age group, seems to bob past him quite naturally, if hazily. Walter had explained it all to him, he tells Abba. ' "You will remember" (he said to me) "how much of her charming company Miss Reich gave us last summer at Cromer when her family were staying quite near"—which charming it was and will be . . . "The time of the great event", he says, "is not arranged, but it will not be yet—not till I can get off a book I am now upon." ' As might have been expected, the 'great deal of work on hand just now' is brought out to delay even such a 'great event'. 'If you can suggest anything in the way of wedding presents', Swinburne goes on, 'I should be very grateful indeed. My addled head can think of nothing.' He has just had a cold, but an addled head seems justified without one. Nine months later, the procrastinating bridegroom had somehow been induced to come out from behind those vast barricades of real or imaginary paper-work, and before long Swinburne was cheerfully winding up a letter of bookish gossip to William Rossetti: 'Walter and Clara—who are also called Mr. and Mrs. Watts-Dunton—send you back their love and regard'. He ordered another present of books for Clara. This time it was a handsomely bound edition of 'Lorna Doone' in which, in his clear, round Putney hand, he inscribed her name 'from her affectionate brother-in-law, Algernon Charles Swinburne'. The 'nearer than a brother' had enlarged the family circle.

The change over to the new order seems to have been managed quite smoothly. We do not know what happened to Mrs. Mason and her sister, except that they continued to come on special occasions such as Christmas dinner at The

Pines. Mrs. Mason hands over the housekeeping keys and withdraws without a single recorded comment that would enlighten us as to how she regarded her brother's marriage. Perhaps she made many, but they seem to have been brushed under the carpet in the general bustle that began, we fancy, as soon as her boxes were carried downstairs and she drove away for ever from The Pines. Yet it must have been a sad abdication. The new young mistress brought changes. We can picture her running up and downstairs from the tower-room to the kitchen, energetically flinging open sash-windows, directing a great banging of brooms and thwacking of rugs, and retiring the ugliest bits of Victorian furnishings. This was, after all, the modern Edwardian age. Before her marriage, she had told Walter playfully, but also half-seriously, that he must really get rid of a particularly hideous Victorian cruet-stand. It was either her or the cruet-stand, she ordered him; the two of them could not be house-mates at The Pines. Clara must have won. Watts-Dunton's friend and biographer, James Douglas, reminisced years later that she finally managed to transform the house considerably. 'Before the marriage, it was crammed with books', he wrote, recalling that there was barely room for two chairs among the mountains of tomes on the floor of Watts-Dunton's study. Clara, he wrote, had 'let in the light and air, and got rid of the accumulated dust and debris of the years'. Swinburne, safe in his own abstracted world, can have noticed little that was going on. It was so deeply insulated that he would sometimes meet Walter face to face among the other ghosts going up and down Putney Hill and pass him without a glimmer of recognition. The bangings and thwackings would be happily muted to his deaf ears. But The Pines, which seemed eternally sunk in the darkest sepia of brown studies, perpetually drowsing like Keats' Autumn on the granary floor of her store of harvested memories, suddenly found herself shaken awake in a season of cheerful spring-cleaning. The day had come, as Clara Watts-Dunton put it, for tidying up. One hopes that the friends were allowed to continue wearing their carpet slippers around the house.

Swinburne's life was the same in all essentials, however. His hours and his habits were the pivot of The Pines, as ever. Walter, the unexpected Benedick, saw to that with his customary care and affection. What, after all, was one young woman more or less in the house if Walter was there, ready to talk, to listen, and to praise—the unchanging rock on which he depended for everything? And he seemed to enjoy Clara's company. It was indeed charming in Putney as it had been in Cromer. He took her walking on the commons to show her his divine May festival of the hawthorns, and she was properly appreciative. He had been accompanied on his walk to-day, he told Walter gallantly when they got home to lunch, by a hamadryad—a positive hamadryad! He admired her less nymph-like efficiency in dealing with intractable household objects which his agitated little hands could never tackle. She even taught Walter to type, but well out of Swinburne's sight. It was pleasant, too, to have a new listener for the sacred readings of Dickens that went on, evening after evening from six o'clock to seven forty-five, week after week, and year after year of his thirty years at The Pines. Swinburne, like Dickens himself, had always loved reading aloud. He had been the moving spirit of the family private theatricals in his boyhood at East Dene. Had he not once acted with gusto the part of Mrs. Skewton in her bath-chair in a version of 'Dombey and Son'? It never struck him for a moment that everyone else might not share his own ecstatic appreciation of his Dickens readings, as it was beyond his imagination that a sane man should not be passionately devoted to infants and to the Elizabethan and Jacobean dramatists, great or mediocre. Walter, patiently listening, had certainly never hinted that his ardour for Boz was less avid.

But Clara—poor Clara! She was young and perhaps not always patient. The tilt of the hamadryad's pretty head, as we regard her photograph, seems to suggest that she would sometimes rebel against living in an old tree, even such a famous old tree. When she was cross, she says, Walter would mis-quote fondly 'Crabbed youth and age cannot live together'. She found the evening recitations inexpressibly trying. She found them a terrible bore. Swinburne chanting his own poetry was one thing. The high, fluting voice rushing along on the great flood of musical sounds had a weird, almost hypnotic effect. It fascinated, even though it exhausted. But when he read Dickens, he felt impelled to act the characters, and he was always breaking off to go into shrieks of laughter after every favourite funny passage. Clara, the gifted amateur actress, listened coldly. Sarah Gamp and Betsey Prig, in particular, threw Swinburne into transports of merriment. He knew them by heart. Gamp-ese had always been the special comic language with which he sprinkled his letters to friends. And Christmas was the worst time of all. Even though there was now no child at The Pines, the Dingley Dell atmosphere was kept up, and it included a perfectly gluttonous intake of Dickens. At the end of the evening, when the Watts family guests who had come for dinner had gone, Swinburne would embark happily on the usual ritual of a reading, to a surreptitiously yawning audience of two, from 'A Christmas Carol'.

Sometimes Clara tried to skip the readings. It is said that when the weather was fine she would go and sit in a little chalet in the garden. Was it the potting-shed which is there today, perhaps more elegantly rustic then, less utilitarian?

It is at the far end beyond the fruit trees. Even through a window wide open on a summer evening, and pitched to the ears of a deaf listener, Sarah Gamp and Betsey Prig might have difficulty in pursuing her to this peaceful countrified corner. Certainly Clara spent more time in the garden than did either of its owners, who preferred to read or work comfortably in their rooms. It was she who planted the old-fashioned rose, Hebe's Lip, where it would throw out its pink-tinged garlands near Rossetti's Venus from Cheyne Walk. But though she escaped whenever possible from the Dickens performances in the early days of her marriage, soon she returned to suffer some more. Swinburne's pleasure in having her as well as Walter to listen was too disarming to resist. Good naturedly, she made herself endure the boredom.

And boring it must often have been, no doubt, for a lively young woman in that strange little household at The Pines. She tried to wake it up a bit by starting to entertain. Now that the stuffy old establishment had a proper mistress, its door could be opened to more than the carefully chosen visitors who were invited by Watts-Dunton to meet Swinburne at luncheon or dinner. There should be a regular, select little *salon*. So we hear of Mrs. Watts-Dunton's Sunday 'At Homes', which drew regular attenders to journey to Putney. The minor literary figures who came to drink tea and talk and eye each other under the scrutiny of the Rossettis were mostly, it seems, Walter's friends and acquaintances. Few of them could have interested Swinburne. If he showed up at all, he sat silent. All the young hostess's vivacity and her husband's kindly welcome may not have made up for the disappointment of guests who had hoped to see and hear the great legend.

The odd *ménage à trois* continued for four years. When Swinburne was alone with Walter and Clara, his spirits were always cheerful, according to her account. Mrs. Watts-Dunton remembered only the happy moments later when, widowed and alone herself, she picked up her pen and wrote about the days with the Bard. Swinburne was the most lovable, child-like of men. Even if he treated them to a flood of blistering invective against something or somebody he disliked, its very extravagance was entertaining. Before the end, she and Walter, and finally Swinburne too, would be in fits of laughter. She recollected all kinds of humdrum small things—that Swinburne's feet, so often described as tiny and fairy-like, were actually a size larger than Walter's, so that Walter often walked away in the Bard's boots by mistake, but the Bard could not squeeze into Walter's. That they were all very fond of roast duckling and ate it frequently. That Swinburne refused to go for fittings to his disapproving tailor, who had to copy a worn-out suit when he needed a new one, and the result was very good. But when she comes to speak of her marriage to old Watts-Dunton, this 'very singular and warm-hearted lady' says simply 'It was a heavenly relationship'.

## XI

THE QUIET remaining years had their moments of excitement. Swinburne's seventieth birthday in 1907 brought glowing tributes in the papers. Letters and telegrams poured in at The Pines. Though he insisted all his life that he was equally indifferent to excessive praise or abuse, the old man was plainly moved and pleased. Lord Curzon, then the Chancellor of Oxford University, wrote soon afterwards to offer him an honorary degree. Swinburne thanked him for the compliment but refused it. He had hated Oxford as much as he had loved Eton, and time had not mellowed his dislike any more than it had softened his loathing of the Romanoffs. His abruptly terminated Balliol career had kept its sour flavour of 'total and scandalous failure'. He had come down without taking a degree. It was a bitter memory, furthermore, that the examiners for the Newdigate Prize Poem had been dull enough to reject his entry—a truly remarkable one—and to award the Prize to a Mr. Latham of Brazenose, who had not been known to utter a poetic syllable since. What effusive nonsense poor Matthew Arnold used to write about the 'sweet city with its dreaming spires'! In Swinburne's irritable opinion, the prevailing atmosphere, climatic and spiritual, of Oxford was always one of 'foggy damp'. She had damply rejected him. And now, forty-eight years later, Oxford saw fit to make amends at last! Oxford proposed that he should put on a gown and walk in procession to hear his life-work eulogized! 'Dear Lord Curzon', he wrote, 'I am much honoured and gratified . . . hopeful that you will not regard me as ungrateful . . .'

A year later, William Rossetti was assured that a rumour of another and greater impending honour was without foundation. He had read a report in *The Times* that, according to the *Svenska Dagblad* of Stockholm, the 1908 Nobel Prize for Literature would be given to Mr. Swinburne. The reply had a brisk snap to it. 'Let me . . . assure you', wrote Swinburne, 'that I have not been offered the honour of taking a back seat behind Mr. Rudyard Kipling.' The 1907 Nobel award for literature had gone to Kipling, a poet from whose work Swinburne studiously averted his eyes, even though the younger man hymned the imperialist sentiments which he shared. When talk turned to Georgiana Burne-Jones' nephew Ruddy at one luncheon party at The Pines, and Watts-Dunton bellowed his name to the Bard, it is recorded that the Bard made a brief and notably grudging comment. All the same, *The Times* report must have fluttered The Pines considerably. Watts-Dunton brightens up and booms some sensible remarks to Swinburne, who passes them on to William Rossetti in the same letter: 'Watts-Dunton says that he thinks it would be a great triumph for free thought, and an infinite service to our common cause: and therefore if ever it were offered me I ought to accept it'. But how could he accept or reject something that was simply air? In that case, Swinburne said with a gleam of the old fun, he would be acting like the monstrously implacable lady who had somehow stayed in his memory from nursery days at East Dene, 'Cruel Miss Baxter, Who refused all the men before ever they axed her'. The offer was not made, and Walter's last hope of seeing Algernon receive his rightful recognition in the eyes of the world faded into thin air with it.

\* \* \*

The iron gate of The Pines went on clanging at the appointed hour, and the shabby little figure, always without
a coat in the worst of weathers, went on speeding up the
hill towards the commons. The worse the weather, the
more delightful it was. Though 'they' would try to stop him
going out, he always felt half-alive if deprived of the precious reviving draughts of wind and rain. Perhaps he covered
his usual four miles to the Rose and Crown and back at a
somewhat slower pace. Everything seemed to be slowing
down a bit. He wrote fewer and shorter letters. No more
arrows were fitted to Apollo's bow. Writing to a friend in
January, 1909, he described himself rather sadly as 'an "idle
old man", like King Lear'. Ezra Pound was in London a few
weeks later, and one of his ambitions was to meet Swinburne. But he wrote regretfully to his father that he had
given up the attempt, since he had been told that the old
poet was now 'stone-deaf and with a temper a bit the worse
for wear'. Mrs. Watts-Dunton's unfailingly sunny memories were, perhaps, not always infallible.

The spring of 1909 was cold and treacherous. Shortly
before Easter, Watts-Dunton took to his bed with a severe
attack of influenza. Clara's mother had died of it a few
weeks earlier. The sacred timetable of The Pines was disturbed in this anxious moment. The evening readings had
to be interrupted, and Swinburne's cheerful suggestion that
he could easily bring the book along to Walter's room was
firmly vetoed. Without Walter, he wandered disconsolate,
at a loose end. Fearfully ill as he felt, however, the invalid
did not forget to worry about what Algernon was doing.
One morning, the weather looked surely far too bleak and
blustery for any walking. He sent a message to say that
Swinburne must not think of going out. But Swinburne had
already left the house. And somewhere on his walk, the last
of the implacable goddesses, the ruthless deities of the

grove, caught up with him and touched him on the shoulder. He submitted to her without a struggle, perhaps with eagerness. The cold caught on his walk turned rapidly to influenza, and then to double pneumonia for the second time in six years. Once more, he was carried down from his bedroom to be nursed in his larger, warmer library. A specialist was called in; nurses arrived, and oxygen cylinders. Strange women to whom he had never been introduced, infernal machines, daring to come into his room! In his lucid moments, he would have fought against them with feeble cries of rage. Most of the time, he lay tossing and muttering deliriously. Clara remembered later how the night nurse had reported he was talking a foreign language. She listened, and thought he was chanting Greek. Was he back in the days of his youth when he loved to recite Aeschylus and to dance round the room as he intoned the choruses like a tiny ecstatic Corybant? Or was he at Bonchurch, walking along the shore and shouting poetry to the gulls?

Wherever he was wandering, the long union, the thirty years journey which he and Watts-Dunton had sat out together, was plainly about to end, and they were not together. By a curious accident, Swinburne was dying as his brother Edward had died, among strangers. Clara's face, we may guess, would emerge only blurred and vague from the feverish dreams—the face of a young person, something to do with Walter, whom he met from time to time on the staircase. The faces that counted were missing if he opened his eyes. Walter was never beside him, nor was Isabel. It was a cruel blow of fate again. Poor Miss Swinburne, distracted with anxiety, was ill with heart trouble, forbidden to leave her bed in her house in Onslow Square. So for the essentially solitary expedition of dying, Swinburne was not to have the illusion of a faithful companion accompanying him part of the way.

Watts-Dunton must have suffered more from the exile at this moment than the traveller did. He had been with Rossetti when his hero of heroes, the best loved of all, had died in the Birchington-on-Sea bungalow. If he ever looked steadily at the possibility of things happening this way, he would have taken it for granted that he would never leave Swinburne's side while he lived. But the influenza virus had mocked at all that. The influenza virus had made nonsense of the devotion of thirty years. He had not been able to put a foot to the suddenly perilous floor of The Pines for ten days. He lay upstairs, weakly obedient to the rise and fall of the thermometer, while Algernon lay dying on the floor below.

And at last, when the doctor's report was very grave, Watts-Dunton could bear it no longer. He asked Clara to help him get up and put on his dressing-gown. Clinging to her arm, he tottered feebly downstairs and disappeared into the library. From the letter he wrote to Isabel Swinburne next day, it seems that Swinburne was conscious and joyfully recognized him. But what passed between the two old men we do not know. Soon Watts-Dunton came out and returned to bed. He said very little. It was the night of Good Friday, and at ten o'clock on Saturday morning, April 10th, Swinburne died.

An unexpected watcher had stood outside The Pines on the Bank Holiday evening. The news on the evening posters had drawn Arnold Bennett there, and the jaunty, chunky figure, with the famous cowlick of hair and the protruding front teeth so beloved later by cartoonists, is the last one we should expect to see palely loitering in the gaslight. He was forty-one, and well on the way to creating that fabulously successful public caricature of a fabulously successful novelist who had come out of Burnley and had London licked. Yet somewhere along the road from the Potteries he had caught the spark from Swinburne. He turns the marvellously acute recording camera under the cowlick upon Putney High Street and photographs it for us, mysterious and unfamiliar in its Bank Holiday transformation, its shops shuttered, only the tobacconists and the pubs at the crossroads below The Pines invitingly glowing, buses and cars rattling by, lovers walking entwined and blind and deaf to all but themselves along the pavements. For there is little left now, except the gardens at the back, to remind Swinburne, if his spirit could again dance aloft and take stock from the leads of The Pines, of 'the outlying (and prettiest) parts of Oxford'. It seems to Bennett, ruminating in the street, strange and negligent, yet somehow 'magnificently human', too, that 'A few yards from where the autobuses turned was a certain house with lighted upper windows, and in that house the greatest lyric versifier that England has ever had, and one of the great poets of the whole world and of all ages, was dying: a name immortal. But nobody looked; nobody seemed to care; I doubt if anyone thought of it'.

Next day was bright and sunny, with life flowing back into the streets and flags flying and Easter flowers, white and yellow, banked in the hawkers' baskets. But 'He was dead then. The waving posters said it'. Bennett notes tolerantly that the great human heart of the *Daily Mail*, alive to the needs of the multitude, had seen to it that the posters announcing Swinburne's death were accompanied by others devoted to some story about a lady and her dog and to news of a lunatic who was going round armed with a revolver. The crowds preparing for the Easter holiday probably glanced at these items with more interest. And that was right, too, for of course the multitude did not remember Swinburne and had never, in fact, known him. He had withdrawn into the solitude of The Pines too long. Yet for very many men, as for Bennett, there was a feeling of sharp personal sadness. Something dazzling and never before seen on land and sea had flashed across their lives and English poetry, and now it had gone forever. The little old man at The Pines was forgotten. It was the fire-bird who was dead.

For Watts-Dunton, it surely seemed the loss of a child. He would never quite recover from the blow. But, still very ill, he had to pull himself together to try and cope with the tragi-comedy of the funeral arrangements. The Abbey had not offered hospitality to the last of England's great poets, as newspapers all over the world were calling him. Perhaps the vengeful shade of the Czar continued to stalk and shake his fist somewhere in the baffling corridors of state where such things are decided. It is hard to imagine Swinburne, if he could have been consulted, agreeing to such an unlikely lodging among the monarchs and the pro-consuls in any case. He was to be buried with his parents and his sisters and brother in Bonchurch. The Swinburne family seemed to take charge immediately, as though they felt that the details of Algernon's journey to their home ground in the Isle of Wight were naturally in their hands. The women in the family, particularly—Miss Isabel Swinburne and his cousin Mary Disney Leith—suddenly appear to us in the fiercely possessive attitudes of mourning women on an ancient urn, standing waiting to bear away a slain kinsman to honourable burial in his own country. And later, when Edmund Gosse began to gather together his material for the biography of Swinburne that Watts-Dunton had been too frail or too hopelessly dilatory to attempt, he would find both these ladies in still more threatening attitudes posted at the door, so to speak, of the sacred tomb, positively forbidding him to enter unless he left certain wicked 'falsehoods' outside. The real Algernon, they would insist, was the great gentleman stretched lifeless within, who had never been drunk in his life, or ceased to be a communicating member of the Church of England, or ever consorted with low-bred women. If the biographer hinted at anything so ridiculous, they promised him that they would not hesitate to expose his fabrications. So Sir Edmund Gosse has told us plaintively in that private memorandum which he later wrote and deposited at the British Musuem, in partial explanation of the discreet reticence of his 'Life of Swinburne'. How could he be seen in public, an eminent man of letters, tangling in ridiculous combat with a couple of fierce elderly ladies?

And now Miss Swinburne, still ordered not to leave her bed in Onslow Square, conducted a brief impassioned opening skirmish with Watts-Dunton, also prostrate in Putney. Neither of them was well enough to attend Algernon's funeral. Clara would go in her husband's place. From behind the barricades of medicine bottles and barley water in their sick-room camps, the invalids despatched letters to each other by messengers who traipsed back and forth across the Thames like heralds negotiating between rival armies. The plump, deeply devout lady in Onslow Square, with her bright blue eyes and her firm mouth and chin, must have expressed herself very clearly. Since Algernon would be buried with his family in the churchyard at Bonchurch, the Church of England would speak the last words over him. Suddenly, though with odd slowness—it must have been the influenza numbing and dazing his still formidable brain —Watts-Dunton recalled his solemn promise to Swinburne that, if he were the survivor, it should not be. After a wretched sleepless night, he wrote, or dictated, the first of two agitated appeals to his 'dearest Isabel'. It may have been the last time that he would feel free to address her with such easy brotherly affection. There was soon to be a coolness between them.

The plans for the ceremony at Bonchurch were out of the

question, he wrote. Algernon's friends would gather, stand silently at his grave, and then go away. 'God knows I would not on my own impulse have told you what I am telling. But I could not rest if I broke this sacred promise. If I should break it I should be miserable all my life. If he had made a slight matter of his antagonism against Christianity, as so many free thinkers do, it would have been different, but with him it increased with his years . . . Pray send me word by your Messenger boy what you have done in this matter.' The word that the Messenger boy carried back to the silent and darkened Pines cannot have been helpful. A telegram, signed 'Watts-Dunton, Sole Executor under the will', was sent off late on the night before the funeral to the Rector of St. Boniface, Bonchurch.

The Reverend John Floyd Andrewes, faced with this authoritative veto at the last moment, quite sensibly settled for one of those British compromises that rarely please anybody but work reasonably well. Mr. Watts-Dunton might be speaking for Swinburne, but the clergyman seems to have felt it incumbent on him to speak as the sole executor of a far higher authority. So when Swinburne's little coffin reached St. Boniface—it had crossed the Solent, sparkling on a glorious April morning, lying on the deck of one of the ordinary Isle of Wight ferryboats, the Duchess of Connaught, and had been saluted with respectful signals from two battleships, the Glory and the Goliath, as the steamer swung out of Portsmouth Harbour—the Rector was waiting to receive it. There was no church service, but he spoke the opening words of the Order for the Burial of the Dead as he walked ahead of the procession to the graveside. He gave a short address. He spoke of Watts-Dunton's telegram, but said that he had 'felt it his bounden duty to pay the utmost respect' to England's great poet who had chosen to lie here in holy ground with the rest of his family, still so gratefully remembered in Bonchurch. Earth rattled on the coffin, the appointed words were spoken, and a *Requiescat in Pace*. To Swinburne's friends, it seemed a shocking breach of faith. The newspapers were full of violent controversy. Watts-Dunton was attacked by angry free-thinkers, who accused him of allowing his friend's wishes to be set aside. For the last time—it would have delighted him—Swinburne himself was attacked in a pulpit. A less charitable Christian than the Reverend Floyd Andrewes, Canon Mason, the Vice-Dean of Canterbury Cathedral, preached there against the notion, put about by a regrettable leader in *The Times*, that Swinburne's poetry had not necessarily led to an increase to sexual immorality. How could *The Times* tell? demanded the Canon. 'There was no more deadly poison than the portrayal of corrupt passion in glowing and artistic language.' In his opinion, he warned the faithful of Canterbury, 'much lustral water and the most precious of all precious blood were needed to do away with the pollution which Swinburne's poetry introduced into English literature.'

Presently the family had the last, or nearly the last, word. The new grave in the high, craggy churchyard at Bonchurch, from which one can see the tops of East Dene's great elms and, on stormy days, hear the crash of the sea, was duly covered, like the other Swinburne graves, with a narrow stone casing on which is carved, as though laid on the breast of a man who has fallen asleep on the turf, a slender Celtic cross.

\*     \*     \*

Watts-Dunton lived five years more. He was the sole heir of all that Swinburne possessed—just over twenty-four thousand pounds, his library, his manuscripts, and his copyrights. He had been a faithful steward for thirty years, and at last his friend could express his gratitude in something more tangible than a dedication. Some people jeered at the promptitude with which he turned many of the manuscripts and letters into cash. After all, he wished to provide for his young wife as well as he could, and there was not much time left. So Thomas J. Wise, Gosse's trusted friend, the well-known bibliophile and dealer, scooped most of the treasures. He and his cheque-book were frequently at The Pines, from which he took away cab-loads of booty, including all Swinburne's unpublished work. Out of these rich hauls he secretly printed a flood of pirated pamphlets for which he omitted to pay Watts-Dunton the copyright fees, and he resold, at handsome profits, much of the Swinburniana, which eventually found its way into the university libraries of England and the United States.

The brief will leaving everything to Walter caused umbrage and division among the living, however, as wills frequently do. There was not a mention of Swinburne's family in it. They were hurt and indignant. From among his belongings at The Pines he had not named even one small personal legacy for Abba or his cousin Mary. It was inexplicable that Algernon, so warm-hearted and devoted, should have acted in this way unless he had been influenced to do so. So the family thought, and Miss Swinburne was said to refer coldly to Watts-Dunton as 'the heir'. The relationship between The Pines and Onslow Square would never return to the comfortable old days of 'dearest Isabel', though he remembered to leave her the Burne-Jones portrait of herself in his own will.

Watts-Dunton became rapidly older and more infirm after Swinburne's death. His mind remained extraordinarily agile. We see Clara pushing him in a wheel-chair along the front at Eastbourne and reading Scott to him in a shelter. The Dickens evenings were dropped, no doubt with a good deal of thankfulness on both sides, but his interest in books and people, too, was as avid as ever. Mrs. Watts-Dunton continued to hold her Sunday 'At Homes' at The Pines, and the old critic enjoyed talking to the guests who were led up to him. Perhaps, if they were tactful, they mentioned 'Aylwin' rather early in the conversation, but their host was keenly interested in all they could tell him, important or trifling, about what was going on in the world. He surveyed a new-fangled dance, the tango, and boomed a not very startling verdict. It would not last! He foresaw with dark forbodings the coming World War—how right he and Algernon had been to mistrust the Germans! He missed Algernon more and more. None of the guests wandering round looking at the Pre-Raphaelite furnishings of The Pines would be likely to see Rossetti as its presiding deity now. In the place of honour over the sitting-room mantel-piece was a huge enlargement of the last photograph of Swinburne, taken when he was about sixty-five by Mr. Poole of Putney. The Bard looks serene and benign, his hair and little beard well brushed, his braided frock-coat immaculate. It was said to be a speaking likeness. Resting on the sofa beneath the portrait one evening in the spring of 1914, Watts-Dunton died quietly in his sleep.

Over a quarter of a century later, Bernard Shaw would pause to look back at the old man dozing on the sofa and speak of him with unusual gentleness. A curious whispering chorus of calumny, most of it proceeding from Edmund Gosse's well-known view of him, had grown in volume after his death. The picture of the dull, vain, and insufferably jealous solicitor who had held Swinburne captive in Putney and taken away his genius, like a warder carefully removing a bright piercing instrument, had become fixed in legend, and it persists even to-day. Shaw laughs at Watts-Dunton, but his laughter is affectionate. 'Watts', he says—for he had 'never picked up the Dunton', to be sure, neither had he known him by the Christian name Swinburne always used —'Watts believed that his sonnets were the final perfection of poetry and his gypsy novels immortal . . . There was a ridiculous side to Theodore; but he was a real good man.' The words echo through the silent sitting-room of The Pines with the ring of truth.

Clara sat alone in the room for many years to come. Watts-Dunton had left her the house and the income from his estate, after the payment of annuities to his sisters, for life. She was still in her thirties and would live on until the eve of another World War. Soon new bustlings and bangings shook The Pines from her tower-room to her basement. Swinburne's books and his remaining manuscripts were taken off to be sold, as Watts-Dunton's will directed, at Sotheby's, and his library became Mrs. Watts-Dunton's bedroom. After all, why not? this practical lady would demand if any visitor to The Pines looked a little scandalized by the change. The books and the poet had gone, and she was the owner now. So she sat at the window where Swinburne had sat, looking down at Rossetti's little Venus, writing her memories and sometimes indignantly addressing the correspondence columns of the newspapers if a particularly unkindly attack on Walter's memory caught her eye. Mr. Clement Shorter's remarks about 'Swinburne's premature senility in that terrible *ménage* at The Pines' was answered in a spirited letter to the *Morning Post*. It ends with dignity. 'I have been content in this letter to protect those who are no longer able to protect themselves, leaving on one side the gross imputation which the paragraph casts also on me as a member of this "terrible *ménage*".' She never re-married, and died in 1938—a dignified end, too.

Watts-Dunton's estate went to his remaining brothers, and a new tenant was found for The Pines. The best of the furniture and pictures followed Swinburne's books to Sotheby's, who sold 'The Artistic and Literary Property removed from The Pines' in March, 1939. In that month, Hitler went into Prague. The welter of painted and padded and gilded and carved objects that looked as though they would stick together forever even though the waters of the earth rolled down Putney Hill seem to rise up in the air, like thistledown blown by the approaching hurricane, and scatter in all directions. The rest of the furnishings were sold by a Putney firm of auctioneers. But by then Swinburne's fame had long begun to wane. The new generation of youth knew him not, or dismissed him as music without heart or thought. He was out of fashion as a poet, forgotten as a man, and the prices fetched at the sales reflected the extraordinary fall. Perhaps his countrymen were too preoccupied at the moment to take an interest in the artistic and literary remains of anyone, however illustrious. Their minds were on air-raid precautions and the plans for evacuating their children out of the cities when war broke out. So the wonderful, funny Chinese day bed coming out of the crocodile jaws of a lacquer cupboard was sold for two pounds five shillings, and the oak cabinet on which Treffry Dunn had painted Swinburne as St. George went for two pounds. Who wanted such things nowadays? Furniture had suddenly become horribly breakable, vulnerable stuff. Rossetti's drawing of beautiful Janey Morris, lying on her sofa arching her swan neck, changed owners for forty-six pounds. And at the Putney sale, the scramble to get Swinburne relics was almost total paralysis. Not a single bid was made for the old-fashioned little brass bedstead in which he had died.

Will the young ever discover him again, I wonder? It could well be so. Swinburne may, after all, have the last word. He went so deep into the lives of the earlier generations who read him that many of them never forgot. Max

Beerbohm, whom we began by accompanying as he walked irresolutely up Putney Hill towards luncheon at The Pines, was one of those to the end. We have Mr. S. N. Behrman's word for it in his tender 'Conversation with Max'. As he and Beerbohm sat talking in the garden of the villa at Rapallo, the old man called his attention to a great tree on the other side of the road below the terrace. 'Do you notice', said Max, 'that on the side facing us it spreads its branches way back, leans backwards—like Swinburne?' Swinburne still walked the earth as a leaning tree. When Max was dying, Behrman says, he took to reading 'Poems and Ballads' again. He read to his Italian doctor, who knew no English:

> We thank with brief thanksgiving
> Whatever gods may be
> That no life lives for ever;
> That dead men rise up never;
> That even the weariest river
> Winds somewhere safe to sea. . .

And even now, when to love Swinburne is to own to being nearly as period a piece as The Pines herself, there must be an occasional passer-by on Putney Hill who likes to stop at her gate, as I do, and look up at her blue memorial plaque, and think of the time when her modest roof sheltered a son of Apollo.

# Bibliography

Angeli, Helen Rossetti, *Dante Gabriel Rossetti, his Friends and Enemies* (Hamish Hamilton, 1949).

Bennett, Arnold, *Books and Persons* (Chatto and Windus, 1917).

Benson, A. C., *English Critical Essays II* (Oxford University Press, 1932).

Charteris, Evan, *Life and Letters of Sir Edmund Gosse* (Heinemann, 1931).

Chew, Samuel C., *Swinburne* (John Murray, 1931).

Douglas, James, *Theodore Watts-Dunton* (Hodder and Stoughton, 1904).

Gaunt, William, *The Pre-Raphaelite Tragedy* (Cape, 1942).

Gosse, Edmund, *The Life of Algernon Charles Swinburne* (Macmillan, 1917).

Hake, Thomas and Compton-Rickett, Arthur, *Letters and Personal Recollections of Algernon Charles Swinburne* (John Murray, 1916).

Hake, T. and Compton-Rickett, A., *Theodore Watts-Dunton*, including *Watts-Dunton and I*, by Clara Watts-Dunton (Jack, 1916).

Kernaghan, Coulson, *Swinburne As I Knew Him* (John Lane, 1919).

Lafourcade, Georges, *Swinburne* (Oxford University Press, 1932).

Lang, Cecil Y. (ed.), *The Swinburne Letters* (six volumes, Yale University Press and Oxford University Press, 1959–62).

Leith, Mary Disney, *The Boyhood of Algernon Charles Swinburne* (Chatto and Windus, 1917).

Lucas, E. V., *Reading, Writing, and Remembering* (Methuen, 1932).

Maartens, Maarten, *Letters* (Constable, 1930).

Moore, George, *Avowals* (privately printed, 1919).

Nicolson, Harold, *Swinburne* (Macmillan, 1926).

Partington, Wilfred, *Thomas J. Wise, in the Original Cloth* (Robert Hale, 1946).

Rothenstein, William, *Men and Memories* (Faber and Faber, 1931).

Steegmuller, Francis, *Maupassant* (Collins, 1930).

Watts-Dunton, Clara, *The Home Life of Algernon Charles Swinburne* (Philpot, 1922).

Waugh, Evelyn, *Rossetti* (Duckworth, 1928).

PUBLICATIONS

*The Fortnightly Review*, June 1909, Gosse, Edmund, 'Personal Reminiscences of Swinburne'.

*The Listener*, March 1957, Noyes, Alfred, 'Dinner at The Pines'.

*Wandsworth Borough News* (contemporary references).

*Wandsworth Notes* (contemporary references).